THE

UNCHARTED JOURNEY

Eddie, Dementia and Me

JACKIE HUCK

2QT Limited (Publishing)

First Edition published 2019
2QT Limited (Publishing)
Settle, North Yorkshire BD24 9RH
www.2qt.co.uk

Cover design by ©Pauline Henderson
Cover typeset Dale Rennard

Printed in the UK by TJ International Ltd

Publisher Disclaimer:
The events in this memoir are described according to the Authors recollection; recognition and understanding of the events and individuals mentioned and are in no way intended to mislead or offend. As such the Publisher does not hold any responsibility for any inaccuracies or opinions expressed by the author. Every effort has been made to acknowledge and gain any permission from organisations and persons mentioned in this book. Any enquiries should be directed to the author.

A CIP catalogue record for this book is available
from the British Library
ISBN 978-1-913071-24-0

Best wishes

Jackie Huck

This book is dedicated with thanks to all those who helped
in any way along this journey.
Also in loving memory of Arty Robinson: Judy Dunford:
Pat Wolstenholme

CONTENTS

CHAPTER 1

BEGINNINGS

We're on a journey to nowhere
on a train we cannot see,
the engine driver's drifting
now there's only me.

The station platform's crowded,
but there's no one really there
spinning round in circles
still sitting in a chair.

We departed without warning
into uncharted lands,
clinging to each other,
two lovers holding hands.

The journey stretches onwards,
no pause or turning back,
emptiness is waiting,
at the ending of the track.

'They've made a grand job of Shap Wells[1]. Is the car outside?' Of itself, not a startling or unusual comment but when it's said by your husband four days into a Mediterranean cruise, it comes as a shock.

Was this the beginning of the journey? Or had we started out a few years before? I suppose the signposts had been

---

[1]   Shap Wells is a large hotel situated in our area (Cumbria)

lying around, I just chose to ignore them. Eddie seemed to spend ages looking for things he'd mislaid, forgot names and became emotional for little reason, but we became good at making allowances, accepting shortcomings, jumping in and protecting him. He was fifteen years older than me so, as he nudged upwards of seventy, I expected age to eventually catch up. He was still active, always busy around the farm or in his workshop, and took pride in people saying he looked ten years younger.

'I'm going to marry her.' He told me later that was what he thought the first time he saw me across the dance floor in a nearby village. It was late November 1975. I was working as the district nurse, with no intention of marrying anyone. He asked me to dance, introduced himself and shortly afterwards we were dating.

I liked him at once but was not 'swept off my feet'. He was taller than my five foot five, with a thick head of blond hair. Years of outdoor work, battling through all weathers with the cows, had given him a healthy, ruddy glow. He was square and strong, with not an inch of fat anywhere. He had large hands from all his strenuous work with machinery and stock, and a gentle smile which reflected his character.

I was to learn that Eddie had many attributes, kindness being the foremost. He had a cheeky sense of humour, was imbued with immense patience, and had a deep sense of responsibility for those he loved. He could rise at five in the morning and, with only a few stops for food, could work through without complaint until eight in the evening, not just for one day but every day without break.

'Come and see my house,' he'd said shortly after we met. I remember him driving me up the lane that evening, the beck bubbling to our right, then into the farmyard, passing the old corn mill that was Eddie's cowshed. Mill House was illuminated by an outside light, which gave the white building a ghostly glow. Built in 1696, Eddie was the third generation of his family to live there. His beloved mother had died some months earlier, leaving Eddie alone; the house reflected his bachelor status.

'I've been doing it up for the last few years,' he said. 'I'm just finishing off the middle room then I'm done.' He showed me round. It was a big, long house, the main rooms all to the front. 'I did most of the heavy work myself but I had to get someone in for the electric, plumbing and plastering. I had to fit it in with the farm work, that's why it took a long time.'

'Your mum must have been very patient.'

He nodded sadly. 'Yes, she was. She never complained but she never saw it finished.'

'I'm so sorry.'

'Come and see the rest,' he urged. We walked along the downstairs hallway, popping into rooms, then up the staircase. 'I altered all this as well,' he said, pointing to another newly plastered area where a door had once stood. The floorboards on the upstairs hall creaked. ' I never got round to the floorboards,' he said. 'I know which ones creak and I used to be good at missing them when I was younger and came in late.' We laughed and I pictured him creeping in, shoes held in his hand, missing the creaks. 'It was open to the eaves at one time,' he said indicating the ceiling from the new green bathroom.

The house was old but endearing. He'd worked hard to make it better; it held charm and had known a lot of love. It ached to be loved again.

We returned to the front room, had a second cup of tea, exchanged background information about our lives then prepared to go. He would drive me home; it wasn't far.

It is a tradition on Christmas Eve in the village that the

carol singers go singing from house to house. Eddie had invited Mum and me over and he'd switched on the old station lamp in the front garden. It was a good evening but there had been a slight sprinkle of snow earlier. We heard the approaching singers and went out together to stand in the front porch while they sang. 'Silent Night' had never sounded so sweet or romantic. From that evening on, the news was out on the local grapevine: Edwin Huck and the district nurse are an item!

Nineteen seventy-six was still newly fledged when I came to The Mill again. By now Eddie had laid the concrete on the middle-room floor and declared his renovations complete. He was no cook but had discovered the delights of ready-made apple pie and tinned custard; this was always my main treat when I visited.

As we sat together, he gave me one of his smiles and a long yearning look as he wafted his hand around the newly refurbished living room. 'It's all here waiting for you,' he said. I'd known him barely six weeks.

The next evening we went dancing. Neither of us was much good; we could just about manage a waltz, a barn dance and some semblance of a jive. We were in the centre of the crowded floor, my head resting on his shoulder. 'The answer's yes,' I whispered as his face lit up with sheer delight.

We were married on 29th April 1976, and Mum and I moved into The Mill. Looking back, the years seemed to fly and I often wonder where they went. We started our own milk round in 1979, bottling green-top milk which was unpasteurised, keeping the round going for twenty-eight years. In the early years we managed an annual holiday when we employed a relief milker. Mum and a village friend looked after the milk round but as they aged holidays became impossible. On reflection, Eddie and I didn't really have much life together over the years; a one-man dairy farm and milk business allows little free time. My mother died in February 2006 and, for the first time since we'd married, we were alone in The Mill. Eddie was seventy-three and had no desire or need to retire.

It had been a poor spring and the cows remained in at night. Late one evening a cow started calving unexpectedly and there was no time to move her up to the calving pen. Eddie rapidly attached ropes to the calf's legs and pulled, as he had on so many occasions. But this time the ropes shot off and he ended up slamming into the cow-shed wall.

Thinking back, I should have taken him straight to the doctor but all he complained of was banging his shoulder and farmers have a bad habit of making little fuss and carrying on as normal. He didn't even have a bruise. The arm was a bit stiff and he found it difficult to milk for a couple of weeks. One of his cousins came to help him out and I rubbed his shoulder twice a day. He never mentioned any other pain and I thought that was the end of the matter.

The summer of 2006 in Cumbria turned out to be the hottest for years. We spent many contented days in the garden and had all our meals out of doors. The weeks wandered on, blissful, balmy weeks of wall-to-wall sunshine. I noticed Eddie was slowing down but thought it was the heat – it was up in the seventies or eighties most days. It was only in early August that I suddenly became alarmed.

We were getting up for the milk round one morning when I heard him tumbling about in the bathroom. He said he was dizzy. Could it be his blood pressure? He was on pills. I made a doctor's appointment and she agreed that it might be his medication. She altered it and everything seemed to settle down. A week later, another milk morning, but this time he just couldn't direct his right foot into his Wellington boot. Try as he might, the foot just wandered around. Alarm bells started to ring; could he have had a slight stroke?

I made an emergency appointment for that afternoon. The GP examined him, didn't think it was a stroke but was insistent that Eddie must go to hospital to determine what was wrong. She wrote a letter to the casualty officer and phoned to tell them to expect us.

It's not easy to drop everything on a dairy farm. Cows must be milked and looked after and the milk still had to be delivered. But farmers are wonderful neighbours and rally round in an emergency. We dashed back from the doctor's and went to see Arty, the farmer at the other end of the village. 'Don't worry, I'll get someone to milk,' he assured us.

Back home, I packed an overnight bag in case it was needed while Eddie marshalled the cows into the milking parlour. We got away to Carlisle at 7pm, after Eddie had pointed out any potential problems to our stand-in milker.

An anxious wait in casualty led to X-rays, blood tests, a full examination and, at 11pm, admission for a brain scan the next day. It was midnight when I eventually headed home, worried sick and exhausted. I remember driving down the motorway then over the moor, picking my way through a sleeping bed of sheep along the road. My faithful black cat, Tommy, was waiting in the gateway and his eyes caught the car headlights as I drove up. He always kept watch if I wasn't home no matter how late it was. I cried myself to sleep that night, praying it wasn't anything serious.

The next day a subdural haematoma was diagnosed, a by-product of the earlier accident; it appeared that Eddie had also banged his head but never told me. This meant he had blood lying on the surface of his brain under his skull. The pressure was causing all the problems and he needed urgent surgery.

Eddie was rushed off to Newcastle, where he had two holes drilled in his skull to drain the blood. It all sounded very alarming but amazingly he made a swift recovery; he didn't even have a headache. It was pointed out to me, though Eddie (who was becoming increasingly deaf) didn't hear, that he did have a large aneurism lying deep in the brain. 'It's not bothering him and he might have had it all his life,' the doctor said. 'Don't worry about it.' All the symptoms vanished and, after a short stay in hospital, Eddie came home to convalesce.

He had strict instructions to take it easy for at least six weeks and this brought on the decision to retire from milking. It was early September 2006 when our milking machine fell silent, and the cows were all sold. It was a sad day, that last milking, and we both shed tears as the cows were driven away.

THE LAST MILKING

Straggling in their usual lazy line,
unhurried, idly munching,
the cows come in to milk
this final time,
packing past the empty calving pens
bottoms bumping,
thumping feet,
the morning tympani.

The cowshed waits,
they crowd the door
stopped as if for traffic lights,
thinking. Nudged along,
they push inside
to claim their stalls,
each recognises her own,
tongues seek water-bowls,
knowing the routine
as the machine begins
its symphony.

The cowshed seems to breathe,
snug with heat and muscle,
overstuffed with flesh,
gentle beasts releasing milk.
Udders drained, they amble out,
a lifetime's work complete.
A hundred feet
crunch away
one by one
the job is done.

We kept the milk round on until the autumn of 2007. Eddie would turn seventy-five that October, a long way past normal retirement age, but farmers are a breed apart from the average worker. There is a phrase 'hefted' when talking about fell sheep who know their stretch of land and don't stray beyond it; they pass on this knowledge to their lambs. Farmers are like that – they are 'hefted' to the land. The land and their stock are part of their souls and they live with the turning circle of the seasons. Most of them want or need little else and, in a strange way, the land keeps them young in mind if not in body.

I was growing weary of getting up on bitter winter mornings, struggling through rain and blizzards. I also wanted us to have the freedom to travel while we both felt able. With this in mind, as we headed through summer I kept dropping broad hints, which were met with either silence or 'let's keep going a bit longer'.

We'd stopped bottling our own milk a few years earlier and were now buying in pasteurised. We were notified of a price rise at the end of August. One morning, as we stacked the crates into the van, Eddie said, 'Well, if we're going to pack in, we might as well do it before the price goes up.'

'What a good idea, love,' I answered with a hidden smile.

After we retired, we crammed eighteen holidays into the next three years to make up for lost time. After being initially hesitant, Eddie eagerly embraced these new adventures with only one condition: 'I'm not flying anywhere.' We went on coach holidays to Scotland, Southern Ireland, Holland, Austria, Spain, the Isle of Man and the Isle of Wight, and we fitted in four cruises. We went to the top of the Eiffel Tower, sailed down the Tagus, walked through fields of multi-coloured tulips, saw the Leaning Tower of Pisa, admired St Peter's in Rome and dipped our toes in the Zuiderzee and the

Mediterranean.

I remember saying to a friend in 2009, 'I'm so happy, I'm afraid.' It's only when the ground starts to slip away beneath our feet that we must finally face up to reality.

There had been one worrying 'blip' in the summer of 2010. We were on a coach trip to Kent and it was the last day of a perfect holiday. On the way back to the hotel, the driver asked if anyone wanted to spend an hour in Maidstone.

'We haven't seen Maidstone,' I said. 'Shall we get off?'

'I'm a bit tired,' Eddie admitted. 'And my legs are aching.'

'Okay, you go back to the hotel and wait for me in the lounge. I won't be long.'

'Don't worry, love, I'll keep an eye on him,' laughed the lady in the seat opposite, who we'd got to know during the week.

Without any concern, I had a lovely hour wandering round the shops. It's strange how some uneventful days turn into landmarks in our lives. I remember being blissfully content as I chose a piece of jewellery I fancied and bought Eddie a palm-tree and fruit-covered shirt for our planned October cruise. There was going to be a themed tropical evening; I could hear him saying, 'I hope no one I know sees me in this.'

The late afternoon sun was still warm as I waited to pick up the coach, which arrived on time. It drew up outside the hotel and I bundled off with the others. I expected to find Eddie chatting in the lounge – he loved a good natter – so was surprised to see him wandering around outside the hotel looking anxious and weepy.

Relieved, he hurried over. 'Where've you been?' he asked.

'Just shopping in Maidstone. It's a lovely town, great shops. You should have come.'

'I'm just glad you're back. Is the car round the back?'

I made a double-take at this statement. 'We're on a coach holiday, Eddie. We're in Kent.'

I took his hand and led him into the hotel. 'Whose house is this?' he asked.

I was starting to feel a rising panic. Whatever was the matter? Was this my fault for having left him for an hour? 'We're staying in a hotel,' I reassured him, 'but we'll be going home tomorrow.'

I got him back to our room and persuaded him to have a lie down. Perhaps he's just tired, I consoled myself.

'As long as the chap who owns the house doesn't mind,' he said.

He slept for an hour. I tried not to worry and he appeared to have recovered when he woke up. We went down to the dining room for the evening meal and it all went away, like a bad dream. I even wondered if I'd imagined it or had made too much out of a few silly sentences. There were no further problems and we had an uneventful journey home the next day.

Should I have taken him to the doctor after we got home? Would it have made any difference? I don't think so. Eddie had no memory of the event; it was my secret.

I suppose I was scared. I'd discovered this wonderful, joy-filled life and I was truly at peace. Was I frightened it was going to be stolen away? I watched him carefully over the next few weeks but nothing similar happened, so I lulled myself into a cocoon of false security. It was just a strange little event of no importance. He was fine. What was I worrying about?

We set off on a seventeen-day Mediterranean cruise on 29th September. This was to be our fourth cruise. We'd enjoyed the others so much – all the wonderful places we'd visited, going to sleep in one port, waking in another, and the sea days just lying around in the sunshine being looked after like royalty by the staff. Exploring all the different areas of the ship and sometimes just standing at the rear watching the bubbling, foamy wake of our ship. Add to this the great entertainment, amazing food and all the interesting people we'd met and the new friends we'd made – it had been bliss!

We had an uneventful journey to Southampton and sipped champagne on deck as the ship sailed at 5pm. We soon sorted ourselves out in our cabin and settled into the by now familiar routine. Eddie was going to be seventy-eight on 3rd October, so I slipped away and ordered a special cake and balloons, and for the waiters to sing at our table on that day.

The first day was uneventful: a calm sea, no wind and a warm sun. I'd always enjoyed sea days, passing through the seemingly endless sweep of the water with just an occasional glimpse of land. We had a leisurely breakfast and wandered around the decks before curling up in comfort on the loungers. Eddie read the ship's daily paper, then had a doze while I read my book. The waiters constantly passed by asking if we required anything to drink and I popped away now and again to bring us back a snack.

I know now that time was running out; I would never be truly happy again.

It was 1st October and we were in the Medina Restaurant, working our way through the five-course meal. The company was convivial and I was relaxed and content.

Without warning Eddie turned to me and said those fateful words: 'They've made a grand job of Shap Wells. Is the car outside?' This brief statement was the herald of the grief to come. Those unassuming words were the door that opened gradually into the abyss from which there was no return.

I assured him we were on a ship sailing away on holiday

and, after a slight look of puzzlement, he accepted it. The remainder of the cruise passed in a blur of anxiety. I watched him with increasing fear, never leaving him alone, and for the remainder of the holiday he 'blinked in and out' of reality.

Thankfully, Eddie's birthday was a great success. Balloons, chocolates and a card signed by the captain arrived at the cabin, which thrilled him as much as if one of his cows had been successful at the Royal Show. The card took pride of place on his bedside table and it remained a valued treasure for the rest of the voyage. His confusion abated for most of that day as we enjoyed one of the on-board lectures and a bowl of chips in the sun around the pool during the afternoon.

It was a formal night so Eddie was in his dress suit, complete with bow tie, and I in one of my posh gowns. His birthday cake was brought to our table in the dining room and ten waiters stood around the table singing 'Happy Birthday', while our table companions joined in. To complete the day, as we were dining the new Cunard ship, Queen Elizabeth, sailed past on her way from Italy (where she had been constructed) to Southampton. We were sitting by a window and had a marvellous view of her. I laughed and said, 'Look, even the Queen has turned out for your birthday.' Eddie told me it was the best birthday he'd ever had, so that was a memory to cherish.

There were a few funny moments. For example, Eddie turned to the chap next to him in the theatre and came out with the comment, 'You'd never believe it used to be a prisoner-of-war camp, would you?' That's what Shap Wells was used for during the Second World War. Most evenings, when we returned to our cabin, he would say he'd enjoyed his evening at Shap Wells but it was good to be home.

One night I woke to see him vanishing through the cabin

door in his pyjamas; he'd lost his way coming back from the toilet. Luckily I was there to turn him round and settle him back in his bunk. I wedged a chair against the cabin door each night after that. Another night I woke to hear water running. I shot out of bed and found he'd left the taps on in the sink. The small shower-room was awash and the water was just about to flood the cabin. As Eddie slept on, I spent an hour mopping up, soaking towels in the miniature lake until I'd dried it all up. I spent the rest of the night awake, worrying, worrying and worrying.

The cruise wore on and his confusion increased daily. Shows were now being held at the market hall in our village as well as at Shap Wells, and he couldn't understand where we'd left the car. When we went to Venice, Eddie was convinced we were in Morecambe; when we arrived in Sorrento he said, 'I haven't seen this part of Blackpool before.' Added to his mental mix-up, his legs were starting to tire and we could only walk for short distances.

On Friday 8th October we docked in Split, somewhere we hadn't been before and I had longed to visit. It was a beautiful day, sunshine and blue skies, with a comfortable warmth. We had breakfast and I had my handbag ready for a trip ashore. I'd put on my thin green trousers as we were going ashore from the ship by tender.

We went for a little walk along the promenade deck but we didn't get very far before Eddie's legs started to ache and he settled down for a rest. It was obvious he didn't want to go anywhere and, since 'It was such a good view across Lancaster', what was the point? I didn't dare leave him to go ashore myself, so we moved to the sun deck and settled down for the day.

I read a book, listened to a tape and, from where I was sitting, looked across to the ancient palace of Diocletian which dates back to the fourth century. I took some photos with a zoom lens but I got no nearer. The day passed slowly. As the tenders returned to the ship, Eddie said, 'It's been a hard morning walking around but I'm ready for my meal at Shap Wells.' That was a strange day.

We muddled through the remainder of the holiday and I started to count the days until I would have him home safe. I read five books and Eddie enjoyed himself in his own way. On one of our last days at sea we went up to the Crow's Nest Bar for the evening, where a group was playing. It was a pleasant atmosphere, quiet chatter and an amazing view over the front of the ship. As we left to return to the cabin, Eddie said he'd enjoyed his visit to Scotland!

So we came back to England. It was cold as we docked in Southampton. Eddie was quite normal that morning; he didn't know where we'd been but he did know it was Southampton and we were on our way home.

I was experienced now at the embarkation procedure and had learned to tie something distinctive around our cases so they were found easily. I'd also recognised the convenience of getting a porter to ferry our luggage to the coach – it was worth a few pounds' tip. On this occasion things didn't quite go to plan because, once we were outside with our porter pushing the loaded trolley, the coach wasn't there. We'd booked with our local travel firm and their coach should have been waiting, but the driver had been sent to the wrong terminal and it took him a while to turn around and work his way back to where he should have parked. Unfortunately this resulted in a wait in the cold. I was so relieved when the coach eventually turned up.

Once on board, all was well. We soon warmed up and the inconvenience was forgotten. We arrived home mid-afternoon; Eddie had shown no sign of confusion all day.

I suppose anyone reading this will say, 'You must have phoned the doctor as soon as you got home.' Yes, that's the logical conclusion but I didn't. One reason was because the weekend was rapidly upon us and there was no emergency to trouble anyone over. Also, Eddie was perfectly okay again; he'd settled into his home and regular habits as if he'd never been away. Was I afraid? Yes, I was terrified. Was I like the ostrich burying my head in the sand? Was it, 'If I ignore it, it'll go away'? Was I being selfish?

I was in the Women's Institute pantomime and I went to a practice shortly after we returned. I left Eddie busy pottering around the farm, back to his old self. Had it all gone away now he was home?

I told my friend Ann, as she drove, what had happened on the cruise. I could see how alarmed she was. 'You'll have to tell the doctor, Jackie,' she said.

The next few days ticked by with no recurrence of the problem. Did I start to hope? Was I a fool trying to pretend it hadn't happened? I lost sleep worrying, tossing back and forth in a dilemma about what I should do.

The decision was taken from me after we'd been home just under a week. Eddie had seemed fine but one evening he gradually became more and more confused. He was sweating and nearly off his legs. I sent for Q-Doc and, by chance, it was our former GP who had left the practice and gone onto the out-of-hours doctors' rota. He diagnosed an acute chest infection, which I was sure was caused by the cold arrival at Southampton. He gave Eddie an injection of antibiotics and a course of tablets. He told me to try to get some fluids into him and to phone the doctor if Eddie became worse during the night or was no better by morning.

Before he left, I took him on one side and confided what had happened on holiday. I can see his face now, that considerate smile as he took my hand. 'As soon as he's over this, get him to the GP,' he said. 'Don't leave it.'

Eddie improved rapidly after the antibiotics; he was able to climb the stairs to bed around midnight and slept soundly until morning. The next day he was fine, though I insisted he rest, and by the following day he was once more out and about around the farm. Even so, I bit that terrible bullet and made an appointment.

'What do I have to see the doctor for?' Eddie asked. 'I'm okay again now.'

'You need your chest checking, make sure all's well,' I lied, feeling sick inside.

We turned up promptly and were soon sitting in the doctor's surgery. 'How's the chest?' he asked, feeling Eddie's pulse.

'Grand,' Eddie assured him.

Eddie's hearing was not good, even with his hearing aid. I lowered my voice and gave a brief outline of the problems during the cruise. Eddie tried to listen but obviously only caught the odd word. 'What you two on about?' he asked.

'Where are you, Eddie?' asked the doctor.

Looking puzzled, thinking our GP wasn't quite right in the head, Eddie answered, 'In the doctor's surgery.'

'And where do you live?'

'At The Mill.'

'Good,' said the doctor. 'And who's this?' he asked, pointing to me.

'The wife, of course, our Jackie.'

'So what day is it?'

At this Eddie looked uncertain, searching for the answer. So far, so good; I had to admit I didn't always know what day it was. Days merge into each other in the country.

'Tuesday? No, Thursday. Yes, it's Thursday.'

'And what month is it?'

Another pause, while Eddie pondered. 'Well, it was New Year not long since, so it must be January. Or is it March?'

'Never mind,' said the GP. 'What year is it?'

'Now, that's a hard one,' said Eddie. '1990? 1996? Well, it's somewhere round there.'

'Have you any family, Eddie?'

'Yes, a sister and a brother. Oh, and Mam and Dad, of course.'

The simple questions continued. For me the world trembled as Eddie talked about his dead brother and parents who were fine and he'd seen recently.

I've often heard the expression 'time seemed to stand still' and now I know how it feels. It's as if the minute stretches to eternity and every heartbeat goes on and on. It's difficult to breathe, to even think; some part of you stops, and words lose their meaning. It feels like an out-of-body experience where you stand looking down on what's happening as a sympathetic observer but you're not the person inside the gathering nightmare. That is how I felt: stunned with the enormity of what was unfolding and totally helpless.

I suppose there was no easy way for the doctor to say it, though illogically I never forgave him for his words. I don't know how he could have said what he had to say any better, but perhaps I expected too much. Did I think he should take my hand? Did I expect tea and sympathy? Perhaps he should have developed a special tone of voice for imparting such news. Perhaps I was basically in shock. I don't know but, as he spoke, I felt as if the ceiling was collapsing on my head, as if the floor beneath me had slipped away and I was falling, falling, crushed by the weight of the words that he imparted in a matter-of-fact voice, as if he were telling me Eddie had developed a cold.

'It's most likely vascular dementia. I don't think it's Alzheimer's, though the symptoms are similar. It's come on quickly so I would expect it to advance rapidly – and, of course, there's no cure.'

Eddie hadn't heard, or if he had the words had no meaning. I was sinking into some sort of bog, sliding away with 'dementia', 'no cure' and 'rapid' hammering into me as I sank. The doctor continued to talk but the words flowed over me as I sat without comprehension, somehow controlling my emotions.

I did manage to ask, 'Is it related to the subdural haematoma he had?'

'I greatly doubt it. The problem will have been developing slowly within the brain for years but it's only now reached the point where it's showing symptoms.'

'So, all's okay?' asked Eddie. 'The wife makes sure I take the pills for the chest but it's really better.'

We shook hands and left with no further words. Eddie chattered on as we walked outside, asking, 'What were all those questions about?'

'Oh, nothing to worry about,' I assured him. 'He was just seeing what your memory is like.'

'Was it okay?'

Somehow I managed to answer in a normal voice, choking back the tears that threatened to overwhelm me. 'Fine, love. Let's go home for a cuppa.'

CHAPTER 2

ABANDONED

As I write this account, I wonder why I'm doing it. Believe me, it's not easy to revisit these memories. Perhaps I hope that by laying down the course of this journey in a simple and hopefully not too dramatic way it might help someone else along the path.

Each journey is different. Although dementia is a standard diagnosis, it affects each sufferer in different ways and the course of one journey can be unlike another, though sadly the destination is the same. So I can only write about the journey that Eddie and I took, my personal feelings, and how it affected my husband in the beginning and as time passed.

It was early November 2010 when Eddie was diagnosed. I somehow managed to drive back home from the doctor's surgery, my mind whirling as he chatted on. I even held some sort of conversation, though my memory of its content has gone. We reached home, had that drink, then Eddie pottered off to his workshop to carry on with some jobs.

I had to tell someone, had to hold someone and weep, or I would scream. I got in the car and went to see Marion, Arty's wife. Thankfully she was in and alone. I vaguely remember walking in; she could see by my face that something was wrong. 'Eddie's got dementia,' I sobbed, before collapsing into her arms, crying uncontrollably. She cried as well as we hung on to each other for what seemed an age but I suppose was only a minute. Then, as I continued to cry, she made hot tea (the eternal remedy) and gathered cake and biscuits. I managed to calm down but was shivering with shock.

'Is there anything they can do?' she asked. I shook my head, the words 'no cure' banging around like a gong in my head. 'I thought there were some modern pills that helped delay things.'

'The doctor never said anything about treatment. He didn't say much really.' Well, he did say something but I was in shock and not taking in the words. What had he said? Something about seeing a consultant? I tried to take my mind back to the surgery, to piece together the blur of meaningless words.

'Eddie will be referred to a consultant just to be sure, to confirm the diagnosis.'

'Is it Alzheimer's?'

'No, vascular dementia.'

'What's the difference?' Marion asked.

As a former nurse I was supposed to know but medicine has made miraculous advances since I gave up nursing forty years before and diagnosis and modern scan techniques have been invented. We didn't really think much about dementia when I was nursing; as people got old some became confused and changed, and sometimes it would state on their notes that they were senile. Also operations and medicines which are now in common use were not available back in the 1960s and 70s, so many elderly people died before they had a chance to develop dementia. But if you have a nursing background you are looked on as the 'font of all knowledge'. I dredged around in my memory of past anatomy lessons, conjured the words – but did I really know?

'The symptoms are very similar and both conditions

cause physical changes in the brain.' I tried to work it out, rethinking my old anatomy classes and recent articles I'd read. 'In Alzheimer's, deposits build up in the brain, killing off those brain cells. In vascular dementia it's to do with the blood vessels, they get clogged up and again those bits die. Eddie's had treatment for raised blood pressure for a long time. It could have been coming on for years.' I hoped that was about right but I wasn't feeling very clinical, just desperate and terribly sad.

'Was his accident to blame?'

'I doubt it. The doctor didn't seem to think so.'

'Does Eddie know he's got dementia?' Marion asked as we sipped tea.

'No, he couldn't hear what the doctor was saying. He thinks he was having his chest checked.'

'Well, I suppose that's one blessing,' said Marion.

Over the next couple of weeks I gradually came to terms with the news. I went through every emotion during those weeks, from the initial distress and worry to blazing anger. Why was I angry? Thinking back, I suppose I felt we'd been robbed of our happiness, like a thief had come without warning and stolen it away.

I kept thinking back over the past few years: the freedom, the laughter, the gentle contentment of shared experience, and the wonderful holidays. Mentally I revisited the places we'd been and yearned for all the places we now would never see, and I just felt so angry, so cheated. I felt angry at the world, at the people around me going about their daily lives as if nothing had happened. Illogically I thought that everyone should feel my suffering, should feel my pain. I wanted to yell, 'How can you just carry on as if nothing's different when the world has changed forever?' Stupid, wasn't it? But that's how I felt. Saddest of all, I felt angry at Eddie as if in some way he was to blame. He was carrying on with his normal life, completely unaware of the diagnosis or how I was feeling.

We'd been having trouble with the television and DVD and, after much hassle and three visits from the TV repair man, had got the thing working. In those early days, I could leave Eddie on his own, especially during the day, and I'd popped into town. When I got home he was trying to watch the news but the picture was black and white with a slight tinge of green, and jumping around all over the place.

I'd been wandering round half in a dream, my mind mulling over the future with gathering dread. Instead of coming home to a quiet relax, I was confronted by the television and Eddie fiddling with the remote.

'What have you done to it?' I demanded.

'Well, I just turned it on and pressed a few buttons,' he answered. He knew we'd almost had the repair man living with us the past week.

'You must have done something.' I snatched up the remote and pressed all the buttons; I even turned it on and off but it was just as bad. I threw the remote down in frustration. 'Why the hell don't you leave things alone? Now you've undone all the good that the repair man did,' I shouted.

At this point Eddie and I had been married thirty-four years and we had truly never had a row. We never raised our voices to each other but always laughed off any problems. Thinking back, I wasn't upset about the TV; that was just the excuse to release some of the anger and helplessness I'd been carrying for the ten days or so since Eddie had been diagnosed.

I stamped around, unpacking shopping, a real 'cow' in a bad mood. Too late I remembered that Eddie's condition was making him not only vulnerable but emotional.

As I turned around, I realised he was crying.

I have never felt so guilty. I wrapped him in my arms, stroking his hair. 'I'm sorry, it doesn't matter. The TV isn't important. I'm so sorry.' Slowly the sobs subsided.

'I didn't mean to muck it up and make you angry,' he apologised in a quiet, broken voice.

'It's me that shouldn't have shouted. It's me that's sorry,' I said, kissing his damp cheek. I vowed in that moment that, no matter what the future brought, that no matter how distressed or frustrated I became, I would never, ever lose my temper or shout at him again. Also, at that moment the anger fell away to be replaced by a deep loving grief that this kind, gentle man was going to leave me, first mentally and then physically.

As November nudged along, Eddie's symptoms advanced. He was usually fine during daylight hours, going about his normal work, busy in his workshop, walling or engaged with one of the many jobs required on a farm. Though he no longer had stock to worry about, the place still had to be kept in order. Helped by John, Eddie kept active. John's sister is married to one of Eddie's cousins and they'd known each other since childhood. A few years before, we'd let John store wood in one of our disused calf sheds and since then he'd been coming up to the farm regularly to help Eddie with various jobs.

During this period I was still able to leave Eddie and go out shopping, to church and village events and to practise for the pantomime, Cinderella. I was playing the White Rabbit (don't ask); Alice, the Dormouse, March Hare, Mad Hatter and I had strayed into the wrong pantomime! We'd been practising since April and there were three performances from 11th to the 13th November.

I grew to dread the onset of darkness. As night closed in,

Eddie's confusion started. He often forgot who I was, called me by many different names and talked about when his mother and father would be home. 'Where's Mother?' he'd ask, before searching around the house trying to find her.

'She's gone out with your Ruby,' I'd say. Ruby was Eddie's sister. That would pacify him for a while.

He also started to lose all concept of time. He'd go upstairs to the toilet about 6.30pm and not return. I'd find him in bed, convinced it was nearly midnight. Then, a couple of hours later, he was back downstairs, sometimes dressed, sometimes in his pyjamas, thinking it was morning. This could occur two or three times in the evening, until I eventually settled him in bed around 1am. I had to fit an evening meal into this hurly-burly lifestyle; not easy. But it was during the night that the problems really became acute.

For a number of years Eddie had always got up once during the night to go to the toilet; this was now extended to anything from four to twelve times. At first I would register the fact he'd gone to the toilet (which was next door to our bedroom) and, in a half-doze, wait for his return. Sometimes he was back after a few minutes but often he wasn't. I would listen tensely, wondering what he was doing all this time in the bathroom, until it became necessary to go and investigate.

Now fully awake, I would wander into the bathroom at perhaps 3am to find him sitting on the toilet seat trying to pull on his socks. At other times he would be fully dressed, convinced it was time to get up. Maybe the bathroom would be empty and I would hunt around the house to find him. One night I discovered him in the front room, curled up in a chair, crying because he was lost. Another night I found him wandering around the downstairs corridor shivering, without a stitch on. He really could be anywhere and in any sort of state.

It became essential that I got out of bed when Eddie did. So began my regular nights of three to four hours disjointed sleep. At times I could get back to sleep straight after I'd got us both back in bed; at other times I would lie awake, listening, mulling, worrying, dropping off just as he was getting out of bed again. As time wore on, I grew so weary trying to exist on these irregular, snatched minutes of sleep.

A short while after the diagnosis, during one of our evening in-and-out-of-bed spells, I made a tearful phone call to Eddie's sister, Ruby. She's a few years younger than Eddie and lives with her two sons, Robert and John. She hadn't been well herself for about eighteen months but was much better, and it seemed right she should know. I just hoped the news wouldn't set her back. She was naturally shocked and upset; she promised to tell the rest of the family and to keep in close touch. She only lives a few miles away, so I said we'd be over to see her soon.

When I'd told Marion about Eddie, I asked her to tell other villagers. I'd also confided in a few close friends. The farming community is a close-knit bunch and, in a small area where most people know each other, it's difficult to keep a secret. It was better that people should know because that way they'd understand what was the matter when they spoke to him. Not that he couldn't hold a conversation; Eddie always enjoyed a chat or 'crack', as they call it round here.

Most of the time he seemed perfectly okay but he could come out with muddled-up memories, talking about people long dead as if he'd seen them yesterday. On one occasion he nearly convinced John that someone they both knew was dead; thankfully John checked, to discover the 'deceased' was fit and well. Also, especially as time passed, there was a possibility of Eddie wandering down the village and getting lost. If people knew the problem, they could always point him back in the right direction.

As the pantomime loomed and evenings became more fraught, I realised it was going to be difficult to leave Eddie. I didn't know how he'd react if he came to the show, even with a friend. We had been out to a few local events but they'd finished early and I'd been at his side the whole time. I warned the pantomime producer that I might have to back out, but at this late stage it would be difficult for someone to step in.

I came to a compromise: my character was only in the first half, then didn't appear until the final curtain call. I got away as late as possible from the house and arrived just in time to be made-up. I did my bit up to my final appearance, about two-thirds through the first act. At this point, while everyone else was either still on stage or getting ready, I bolted off.

It was about a twenty-five minute journey and I managed to make it home around 8.30pm. I was told there were a number of comments from the audience: 'Where was the White Rabbit at the curtain call?' Some thought I'd had an accident or been taken ill, but anyone who asked was told that my husband was ill and I had to get home.

The first night when I returned, Eddie was sitting watching TV in his pyjamas. He'd been to bed and come back down, and he just couldn't understand where I was. I made us drinks and a snack and told him about the pantomime. He eventually went to bed around 11pm.

After my usual three hours' sleep, I worried for most of the next day but went through the same procedure that evening. This time when I arrived home he was sitting in bed with the light on, clutching a rolled-up newspaper. 'Thank goodness you're home! There's been all these people around and I don't know who they are,' he said.

I tried to reassure him there was no one else in the house but we had to walk room by room before he was convinced. I truly wondered if I dare leave him for a third evening.

The next morning I went to see Marion and it was agreed that Arty would come and sit with him for the evening. For the final performance I could stay until the end, enjoy the last curtain call and the speeches.

Arty hadn't arrived when I was ready to leave. I hung on as long as I could then, assuring Eddie that Arty would be there any minute, I left.

I enjoyed the first relaxed evening I'd had for a while. The panto went well and the applause was long and genuine. It was a grand evening. We all agreed the long months of practice had paid off and, as the curtain fell for the last time, we felt it had been worth the hard work.

I arrived home around 10.45, expecting to see the lights on, Arty's car outside and to find the two men sitting chatting or dozing by the television, but all was in darkness.

The door was locked and every light was out. I decided Eddie must have wanted to go to bed and Arty had left early but, when I went up to the bedroom, Eddie's bed was tussled about and he wasn't there. Starting to panic, I rushed back downstairs and into the front room; to my relief, Eddie was sitting in an armchair in the dark.

I put the light on. 'Where's Arty?' I asked.

Eddie was in a combination of night and day wear; he had on his outdoor jumper, pyjama bottoms and one sock. 'He never came.'

I couldn't understand what had happened as Arty was so reliable and knew the problem. Surely he would have come? Eddie interrupted my thoughts. 'I've been up and downstairs all evening but he's not here. There's been loads of other people coming in. Don't know who the hell they are, so I hid in the bedroom for a bit.'

Just then the phone rang; it was Arty. He'd arrived a few minutes after I'd left but found the house in darkness and all locked up. Repeated bell ringing had brought no response and he'd been worried sick. He'd returned a few times during the evening and even sat outside in the car, but in the end he'd given up and decided to check all was okay when I got home. I assured him Eddie was fine, apologised for the worry and thanked him.

'You must have put out all the lights, and gone upstairs right after I left,' I said to Eddie.

'No, I sat around with all these strangers for ages, but in the end I thought I was safest in the bedroom,' he assured me.

I told him it didn't matter; it was over now and I was home. I got him up to bed. 'Did you enjoy your night out with Doreece?' he asked as I settled him down.

Doreece was my mum, dead four years. 'Yes, pet, we had a lovely evening.'

'Oh, that's all that matters,' he said. He turned over and was soon asleep.

***

I've called this chapter 'Abandoned' and in a strange way that's how I felt. When I'd got my head together after the diagnosis, I phoned the doctor's receptionist to confirm that an appointment would be made to see a consultant but, because of the waiting list, it would be the New Year before he would be seen. Also, a brain scan had been ordered. These were positive steps but they were all to confirm the diagnosis; no practical help or advice was given or offered at this stage. I didn't even know if there was anything available; I just had the impression from the doctor, right or wrongly, that, well, it's sad, but that's the way it is. There's nothing to be done, so go away and get on with it. So that's what we did.

November slipped into December and Christmas started to loom. I have a vague memory of going through the motions, writing Christmas cards and letters, buying presents, preparing for the annual 'food siege', when it feels like the shops are closing for a month and we stock up with every imaginable provision and end up with over-stuffed cupboards and fridges. Of Christmas itself I have no memory at all; I suppose it must have been uneventful.

Life was settling into this increasing nightmare of little sleep and continual worry. I was now leaving Eddie alone only occasionally after dark and then for no more than an hour. Wherever possible I took him with me if I went anywhere, or I just didn't go. To enable me to continue going to the monthly WI meeting, where at the time I was the secretary, Arty came and spent the evening to keep Eddie company. We had it sorted now and he always arrived before I left. He was a treasure, and he allowed me to keep this one special lifeline open for a number of months.

I found it difficult to explain to anyone how the dementia was affecting Eddie. To the casual observer he seemed unchanged, still with his healthy outdoor, farmer's glow, still smiling and chatting as he always had done. If anyone asked 'How's Eddie?', I'd say, 'Oh, he's okay, just a bit muddled.' But this was my face to the world. No one saw me tumbling out of bed, time after time during the night. No one saw me turning round and round in bed after being disturbed, trying to snatch some sleep before the next tumble out of bed. No one heard me crying with tiredness and despair when I was alone.

I suppose I should have kept a diary through that first year, but I've never been a diary keeper. I did keep the calendar, which highlights important appointments, and I also jotted down a few notes. Thinking back as I draw these memories together, the timeline becomes blurred.

I remember many events, the peaks and the lows, the funny incidents and the saddest, but their chronology becomes confused. I therefore tell this story as best I can, trying not to put the cart before the horse. I suppose it doesn't matter; it's the progress of that year that's important, the gathering crisis as the snowball that rolled along grew larger and larger as the months advanced.

My most vivid memory of January 2011 was the cold. Eddie was about the same; the only noticeable change was his mobility, which became very variable. At times he was fine, but on other days his gait was unsteady. If we went out, which wasn't often during that winter, I realised on a bad day that it was impossible for him to walk any distance. He would start off okay but after ten yards he'd start to slow down and feel wobbly.

The house is centrally heated but this was provided by a Super Serve Rayburn that runs all the radiators and heats the water. If the Rayburn is not on, or goes out, the heating goes off. We did have electric fires but not only are they costly but, with a big room, one or even two bars of heat doesn't do much good. In past years Eddie had always been in charge of the Rayburn. We'd discovered shortly after having it installed that it was far better to let it go out at night and re-light it in the morning. If we banked it up overnight it took a lot of fuel, plus it still needed raking out to the dregs in the morning or it would be dead by afternoon. Suddenly this regular daily task became impossible for Eddie, so it fell to me to keep us warm.

My day now had to start with cleaning out yesterday's

ashes and taking them round the back. Then fuel had to be gathered and the Rayburn relit. The coal was easy to collect as it was just around the back of the house, but sticks and logs (which we used more than the coal) were a different matter. Eddie always used to chop sticks daily but he had to go down to his workshop to do this. The snow turned to ice, and outside the door and down the farmyard became a hazardous skid slope. He tried a few times to venture out and twice he fell, luckily in the snow so he didn't hurt himself, and he managed to get up with a struggle. Terrified he might fall and break a hip, I insisted he stay indoors and leave it to me.

Our elderly neighbour took me down in his Land Rover to the village shop to stock up on necessary groceries and bags of sticks, so that was the stick problem solved. Logs were a different matter, as these were stored at the bottom of the yard in the old cowshed. After the previous icy winter, I had invested in a pair of expensive boots which were specially designed to grip on ice. These now became a godsend as I made at least eight or nine journeys up and down the yard carrying armfuls of logs back to the house. This might sound like unimportant, tedious detail but little things become significant when suddenly the normal pattern of life is thrown into turmoil. Other women in a similar position can suddenly find that heavy tasks, usually carried out by the man, are forced onto them. Some will have family to help but families are more scattered than they were in the past; that leaves you and somehow you must cope.

I don't look upon myself as a weak woman but I am the first to admit I have neither the strength nor the stamina of a man, plus I've suffered with rheumatoid arthritis for nearly ten years. I am quite able to carry out most day-to-day tasks, but I recognise my limits and exceed them at my peril.

I know I could have asked John or other friends and neighbours to help and they would have, but I felt that their help might be needed far more later on. While I could manage, I should try. So, thinking back, I picture myself up and down that yard, fighting wind and blizzard, treading carefully in my amazing boots and managing on a daily basis to 'bring in the logs'.

As January advanced, John dug and gritted a path for the car so I could get down to the shop. He also stayed with Eddie while I drove into town. Thankfully the bulk of the snow melted over the next couple of weeks but then the rain set in; it was unpleasant for the daily log haul but at least it was safer underfoot.

It must have been sometime in January that Eddie went for his scan, though I remember little about it. Also, as January drew to a close, we took our next step into dementia.

The confusion, which had become a regular part of our evenings and nights, now began to kick in at any time. There had been small blips in the past few months but these were infrequent. Usually Eddie was fairly normal in daylight hours but from the onset of February it happened almost daily.

His appointment to see the psychiatric consultant was on Thursday 3rd February at our local hospital. It was a fine but cold day. The car park was so full, we had to park outside the DIY shop across the road. Eddie was having a good day with his legs and we managed the walk across the road.

'Who're we going to see?' he asked.

'A special doctor,' I answered.

'Why?'

'Well, your memory's getting a bit bad and you get muddled up.'

'Do I?' said Eddie, surprised. 'I won't have to stay here?' he asked, worried.

'No pet, we won't be long.'

We found our way to the correct department and were shown to a relatively new area of the hospital. After a short wait we went into see the consultant, who was kind and understanding. He had a letter from our GP and at first he just asked me for a few background details. Then he sat Eddie close to him and, as I took a back seat, he delved into his memory.

It appeared there was a hundred-question formula. Thinking back, I was both fascinated and worried. Searching through my memories, I recall basic questions about Eddie's life; he answered these well, especially if they were about his childhood. As we came up to date, the answers became vaguer and sometimes were mostly guesses. There were word games, where Eddie had to fill in missing words, pictures where he had to name what he saw, and memory tests when the consultant said words then asked Eddie to relay them back. There were a few simple sums, both on paper and without, and a clock face to tell the time.

I listened, knowing I must not interfere but wanting to jump in and help when Eddie got stuck. I'd put new batteries into his hearing aids and advised the consultant about his deafness, so he spoke slowly and distinctly. I know that Eddie heard but he obviously didn't always understand. Sometimes he had to write things down and it was only at this point I realised Eddie had almost lost that ability.

The tests must have taken about forty-five minutes but it seemed longer. After each section, the consultant recorded a score. He added them all up at the end.

Finally, after thanking Eddie, the consultant turned to me. 'The optimum score for this test is one hundred and anything below eighty-five gives cause for concern. Your husband has scored sixty-five. I'm almost certain it's the vascular type of dementia, and it's well advanced.' He said the words gently, his smile comforting, knowing their impact.

'Is there anything that will help?' I asked.

'We can try some medication. It might improve things a little but the aneurysm could cause problems.' He referred to the scan. 'It's lying in the optic chiasma. One day it might affect his sight. I'll also put in a referral for a psychiatric nurse to contact you. She'll liaise between you both and myself.'

'It's worse after dark,' I said, 'though he can get confused during the day.'

'That's fairly routine. Keep everywhere bright. Try to cut down on any clutter. Plain walls and furniture help, and pictures on doors like a bed on the bedroom door. And keep items around that hold memories.'

'How did I do?' asked Eddie, who'd been trying to listen. I always felt uncomfortable talking about Eddie in front of him when I knew he couldn't hear; it was his life, his condition, but unfortunately it was my worry.

'Fine, Eddie,' the consultant assured him. 'We all forget some things as we get older.'

'I remember most things well. I was having a chat to Mam the other day and we had a real laugh about when we all used to go off on picnics when me, Bobby and Ruby were small.'

'Do you think the summers were better then?'

'Sometimes, but we could have a real struggle getting the hay in. It was no sooner dry than it rained again. It could take six weeks and it wasn't really worth feeding at the end. When it was really hot, we had to start early as it was hard work on the old horse.'

'They're good memories, Eddie. It's been nice chatting to you,' said the consultant as they shook hands.

I thanked him. 'You're doing well,' he said. 'You're both doing well. I'll be in touch with your doctor about the medication. Let's hope it slows things down – it might.'

We drove home, my mind once more in turmoil, but I had a couple of straws to clutch onto. There were some pills that might help; they weren't a cure but perhaps could slow the dementia down, calm things for a while. Surely this was a small glow of hope? Also, there was going to be a nurse; someone would come to the house, a solid, understanding shoulder for me to lean on.

From Eddie's point of view, we'd had a trip to see a doctor, a nice chap who asked a lot of daft questions. 'Daft' became one of Eddie's favourite words as his vocabulary gradually narrowed. He had no idea why we'd wasted the afternoon. He was glad to get home for his afternoon tea and was soon down in his workshop.

The next day was a beast in more ways than one. The rain lashed down continually and a gale raged outside; indoors a different gale called confusion was raging.

I'd struggled to sort out the Rayburn and we'd had breakfast. Eddie was reading the paper. I often wondered how much he actually read as he got through it pretty quickly. I think he read headlines and looked at the pictures; I don't think the content of the various news items meant much to him.

***

He settles down to watch TV as I busy myself around the house. He's standing with the side door open, coat on, heading out into the rain when I come downstairs.

'Where you off, love?' I ask.

'I've got to sort out the pony.'

'What pony?'

Eddie looking puzzled. 'The one I bought earlier, from

those two girls.'

'Which girls?'

'They came to the porch. It's a nice pony. I'm off to feed it.'

'I'll get my coat and come with you,' I say, dashing to get coat and Wellingtons. Off we go into the deluge, battered by the wind. My hair's soon soaking, clagged like wet grass to my head.

Eddie grabs a bucket and fills it with water as we go into the top barn, which is now a wood store. The water in the bucket slops around as he goes from stall to stall. 'Where's it gone?' he asks, hunting.

'There's no pony, Eddie,' I say.

'Of course there is, it's a brown-and-white one. It must be thirsty and it's going to need some feed.'

'Really, Eddie, there's no pony.'

He shakes his head, frustrated. 'It must be down in the other shed.'

Back out into the storm, splashing through puddles, now facing the rain which stings our eyes. Down the yard to the old mill buildings which had been our cowshed.

'They must have left it in here with the cows,' he says, lifting the latch. The cold, empty byre, devoid of cows for three years, opens up into silence and darkness. 'Where's the cows?'

'There are no cows, they went when you retired,' I answer, gradually getting wetter.

'They must be out,' he assures me. 'That's where the pony must be, out with the cows in the fields.'

I change tactics. 'Well, it'll be okay then, it'll be eating the grass and it can get a drink from the stream. Let's go back in the house, out of the rain.' Unconvinced, he allows me to take him back into the dry.

We've been back in the house an hour. I've about dried out and warmed up, when Eddie goes to the front window. 'When do we leave?' he asks.

'Are we going somewhere?'

'We've got to go down to the cottage.'

'Which cottage?'

He turns from the window, exasperated. 'Don't be daft, Jackie, we can't be staying here. This is where Norman lives. We've got to be off.'

'But, we live here.'

'No, we don't, we live at The Mill.'

'This is The Mill.'

He starts to laugh. 'You're going daft. This isn't The Mill. Come on, we'll have to be off.' He heads for the door, grabbing his still-wet coat, pulling on Wellies. I'm back in a coat but there's no time to put on Wellingtons as I'm running to catch up with him, my shoes filling with water as he splashes off down the yard.

I catch up down by the old cowshed. 'Really, we're at The Mill.' I turn him round and recognition of his home dawns.

'So, we're back from the cottage,' he says. 'But where's Norman?'

I refrain from asking who Norman is. 'He's gone,' I say.

Satisfied Eddie heads back into the house, we dry out for the second time.

***

Most days from now on followed a similar pattern plus, as far as Eddie was concerned, the house and garden were always filling up with people. One fine afternoon a few days later, I found him with the front door open chatting and laughing. He turned round to me. 'They're all lost,' he said.

'Who?' I asked.

'All these actors from Coronation Street. They arrived by coach and they've been wandering around the garden. I better go and show them the way down the village.'

I watched discreetly as he proceeded to direct this invisible crowd back down the yard. He waved as they headed off. Smiling, he returned. 'They were a nice bunch, not a bit stuck up. I've put them back on the right road. They should find their coach.'

The next morning it was a group of chaps in a Land Rover who were parked in the front garden, and he spent all afternoon asking me when Doreece was coming back from town.

Since the nights were still a regular merry-go-round and the days were no better, I seemed to be in a continuous spin. Surviving on my three hours of disjointed sleep, and waiting each day for the next bout of confusion, I waited to hear from the doctor, hoping the promised 'magic pills' would soon be prescribed. Where was the soul-saving nurse?

As I've already said I didn't keep a diary, but I did write some notes, including the following.

***

Saturday 12th February 2011. 1.30am

The full impact of yesterday has only really just dawned. Well, it started to dawn at 12.30am, when Eddie went off for one of his regular bathroom voyages. I left him for a minute then popped in to see what was happening. He was in his outdoor moleskin pants and thick jumper. 'I didn't want to wake them up,' he said. 'I thought I was being so quiet.'

I didn't ask him who 'they' were as I peeled off his jumper and pants and got him back into his pyjamas. He was soon back in bed. So, I tossed and turned over twenty times and decided to come downstairs. It was then the full impact of yesterday hit me.

Having not heard from our GP, I phoned the surgery. 'Have you received a letter from the consultant?' Oh yes, they had received it.

I stressed that the consultant wanted Eddie to have a new pill, and he should be starting on it as soon as possible. She'll get the doctor to phone me back. Should I make an appointment? No, he'll phone.

He does phone an hour later. It's the new chap; he sounds nice, but he's a stranger. He's discussed the consultant's suggestions for the medication with our usual GP and they both agree that the side effects far outweigh any minimal advantage.

'So he won't be put on them?' I said.

'No, in view of the aneurysm he could have a serious bleed or have bad gastric problems.'

So − that's it, I think. But it doesn't really make a real impact, not then. 'What about the nurse who was to contact me? I've heard nothing.'

'Oh, that will be the psychiatric nurse. They'll have just got the letter. If you haven't heard in a month, let us know.'

I thank him, and put down the phone and it just floats around, a spider spinning a thread, until the early hours of the morning.

So that's it! No further treatment − nothing! Zilch! The GP reminds me of Pontius Pilate; he's carefully washed his hands and turned away. There was no inquiry, no: 'How is he?' 'How are you coping?' 'How do you feel?' 'Do you need anything?'

Am I being unfair? Perhaps, but it's 1.30am and I don't expect I'll get much sleep tonight, or any night, and I don't feel particularly fair.

It's 1.50am and I'm still downstairs. I've made a hot chocolate and written this. I'm feeling empty, discarded and so alone. But, since there are no magic pills which might slow down this journey, and for the time being no kind, soothing nurse will come galloping up like a knight in shining armour to listen and help, that leaves me and Eddie drifting onwards into the unknown.

I feel like a small boat cast away on a massive lake or ocean, with no oars or rudder. Abandoned to whatever fate has in store, cast off into the empty, cruel void of dementia.

CHAPTER 3

ANEURYSM

I debated whether to include this chapter as in some ways it strays away from the central theme, but it was part of the journey. Also, it must not be forgotten that many dementia sufferers have accompanying complaints. In Eddie's case, he had high blood pressure, thankfully under control, and angina. He could go six months without resorting to his heart spray, but he had been rushed to hospital once with a suspected heart attack, plus he was deaf and had the aneurysm.

Other patients can have a wide-ranging array of ongoing complaints, from arthritis to cancer; just because they have dementia does not exclude other conditions. The main trouble is that the problems are doubled because of the dementia. I think that the medical and nursing profession have only recently awoken to the need to understand the special and different care required when someone is seen as an out-patient or is admitted to hospital with dementia added into the mix.

A dementia patient, depending on the stage of their illness, can find it difficult or impossible to understand explanations. If they do take in some information, a short while later it is forgotten. If admitted to hospital, the patient can rapidly become disorientated, is prone to falls or wandering, or can do something that is deemed unacceptable behaviour. Often they can't even remember their relatives, so they are unlikely to make any connection with a nurse or doctor no matter how often they see them. Simple instructions can mean nothing, and they easily become fearful or agitated in an unfamiliar environment. They run a high risk of dehydration and malnutrition, especially if they are not carefully monitored, plus they will routinely tear out intravenous drips, feeding tubes or refuse medication. All these problems are understood in specialist units, which deal with dementia on a daily basis, but do not readily spring to mind on an ordinary hospital ward.

When Eddie's long-standing aneurysm started to cause trouble, dementia compounded the problem. It also cast me onto a roller-coaster ride of emotions. I suppose this chapter is as much about my reaction to the situation as to the impending threat to Eddie, as I suddenly discovered there was a chance he could go blind!

After my 1.30 am prowl around the house on the 12th February I returned to bed, but was disturbed five more times that night. I had to be up at 6.30 in the morning as I was helping the WI at the farmers' market. I got Eddie out of bed and sorted, stumbled through breakfast and arrived at the market hall at 8am. I dread to think how I looked; if it was anything like I felt, it must have been pretty bad.

I thought I had gathered my emotions but the moment the other girls turned up and asked me how I was, the floodgates opened. I felt better after a quick howl and settled into the general work of serving teas, bacon rolls and cake. Once the initial dam had been plugged, I faced the world that day with little or no sign of the distress of the previous night.

Mid-morning, a friend popped into the kitchen to tell me he'd just steered Eddie back to The Mill. 'He seemed lost, but he was walking back up your drive last time I saw him so he should be okay.'

I thanked him and decided I'd better dash home to make sure all was under control. I slipped outside to head home (only a three-minute walk) but saw Eddie wandering around the market. He looked scruffy, wearing his old tractor jacket which he must have grabbed against the cold.

His face lit up when he saw me. 'I was coming to find you,' he said. 'The house is full of police and I want a bath.'

'Well, if the police are there they'll take care of things. Let's you and me have a cup of tea,' I advised, guiding him into the market hall supper room. 'Whatever are you wearing?'

'I couldn't find anything else. I think the police or them other chaps must have pinched my other coat,' he said, as he drank tea and enjoyed a piece of cake. 'Where's our Bobby? He was around earlier?'

'He's gone back home,' I said. I'd given up reminding him that his brother had been dead for a few years. We spent the next quarter of an hour chatting about what Bobby had been up to. His brother, wife and family had lived in Leicestershire for many years, though Eddie and I had only been three times, the final time to Bobby's funeral.

It was only twelve noon, but the market was quietening down with it being February. The other WI helpers understood there was no way I could leave Eddie and that I needed to take him home.

We walked back through the gathering rain. Eddie said, 'I don't remember this part of town. Does our Bobby live up here?' It was the last time I helped at the market, and another door became firmly shut.

Since he was determined he wanted a bath, we sorted that out in the afternoon. He could still just about manage to get in and out but it was becoming more difficult for him to keep his balance. Afterwards, since he was now convinced it was bedtime, he went to bed, but he was up and padding around in his pyjamas a couple of hours later. It was a fraught evening with him back and forward to bed three or four times.

He woke at 1.15am the next morning but instead of going to the bathroom he sat on the side of the bed. 'We must get the police,' he said, becoming distressed. 'They've stolen the cats and put them in the back of a hearse!'

I tried to assure him the cats were fine.

'But I saw them,' he insisted. 'They were siphoning off the diesel and stuffing the cats in the back.' He'd obviously had a dream which had become real.

I made him a warm drink and after a while he calmed and went back to sleep. This was the first night that Eddie became incontinent, most likely caused by all the upset, but it was to become an increasing feature as the time advanced, just another step along the journey.

In all the years we'd been married, Eddie had never forgotten to buy me a Valentine card. I knew he would be upset if he realised on the 14th of February that he had no card, so the week before I'd taken him to the shop to choose one. By the morning of Valentine's Day, he'd lost it! We had a mammoth search and discovered it tucked in a pocket of the car.

I brought him a pen, sat him down and he struggled for the next ten minutes to write it. He managed his name and a few kisses. 'My writing's getting awful,' he said, 'but I think you can read it.' He also produced a red rose that he'd bought at the same time but he had kept this safe in his workshop. How I treasure that card.

I'd made an appointment for myself to see our GP on Tuesday 15th to clarify the phone call of the previous

Friday, which had caused me such distress. I went with the intention of giving him a piece of my mind since I'd had no contact with him since October. I ended up just sitting in the chair and crying, not helped by the fact that it was the fourth anniversary of my mother's death. He reiterated what the new doctor had told me on the telephone. He was perhaps slightly more consoling than during our previous encounter – well, I was sobbing the whole time. Yes: it was a severe form of vascular dementia. No: there was nothing to be done, it would just take its course. Yes: I would hear eventually from the psychiatric nurse and he would try to hurry up the appointment. So that was that!

The s… hit the fan on Friday. It was the 18th but it felt like it should have been Friday the 13th. Eddie had a planned appointment to see the optician. He'd been complaining for a few weeks about it 'being dark' when he was trying to read the paper. I'd put a reading lamp over his chair, which seemed to improve things, but it had been a while since he'd had new spectacles.

I explained to the optician that Eddie was deaf, so he spoke quite loudly and slowly as he carried out the eye test. First one eye then the other, the customary performance with the metal frames, lenses and the alphabet chart. It rapidly became clear that something was wrong. With one eye, Eddie struggled to get three rows down the chart; with the other eye he had trouble right from the top. Other tests followed, none with good results.

'His eyesight has deteriorated vastly since his last test,' said the optician. 'He's not seeing much on the right side and his vision is reduced on the left.'

'Could it be something to do with the aneurysm?' I asked. 'The consultant said it was lying in the optic chiasma and it might eventually cause problems.'

'I'm sure that's the cause. It's obviously pressing on the optic nerves.'

I'd been getting more alarmed as the eye test had continued but now I felt physically sick. I was back in the doctor's office, that first terrible day when he'd first said 'dementia'. That same trembling, that same quivering unreality, as if the world was spinning on without me and I was just hanging suspended in a black hole.

'He needs an urgent referral to a neurologist,' said the optician. 'I'll phone the hospital and see who the duty neurologist is.'

I sat there while he phoned. Eddie was out of the 'special chair' and sitting beside me, the gravity of the situation beyond him. I felt as if I were drowning. Eddie was deaf, rapidly losing his mind and was now also going blind.

I fought against the tide as Eddie chatted on about something. I just nodded as the waves washed over my head. The optician was speaking to the neurologist; the call lasted a few minutes and the medical terminology sounded long and serious. The optician thanked him and put down the phone. 'I'll write a letter to your GP. He must send it immediately to the neurologist who'll make him an appointment early next week.' Yes, this was a pressing problem – literally. The NHS can move swiftly when required.

Fifteen minutes later, we were back in the car with the letter heading directly to our doctor. That meant a swift dash up the A6 to get there before surgery finished. I felt like I should have a police escort, or at the least a siren. I drove on automatic pilot, a woman on a mission.

Eddie waited in the car when we arrived as I rushed into the quiet surgery and thrust the letter at the receptionist. She knew about it; the optician had phoned, and yes, they'd send it at once. 'You should receive a phone call from the neurologist's secretary in the next few days,' she assured me.

I must admit not feeling exactly optimistic at the time about 'a swift appointment'. Since it was already Friday, and most hospitals go into 'recess' at weekends, I thought I'd be lucky to hear before the end of the following week. With this and many other thoughts churning round my head, we drove home.

Eddie had a good day on Saturday. This was the strange phenomena at this stage of his illness: he could be perfectly normal for hours on end, no confusion, just carrying on his regular life. On these days he'd busy himself around the farm, perhaps doing some walling, tidying a shed or repairing something. Anyone meeting him would have no idea anything was the matter; he could hold a perfectly clear conversation – but he could also suddenly 'blink' out. He might call me by another name, or perhaps set off to find non-existent stock, then just as quickly he'd 'blink' back and return to normality. We'd had no 'blinks' at all that day, and in the evening we went down to a turkey-and-ham supper at the Methodist Chapel room in the nearby village. We had a lovely evening; I managed to relax and Eddie chatted quite happily to old friends.

As so often happened, a good day led to a bad night. Because of Eddie's unpredictable incontinence, I'd bought a protective waterproof covering for the mattress, and invested in a number of cheap bedsheets. I'd also purchased quite a few extra pairs of pyjamas. I was now finding increasingly that I needed to both dress and undress him. Left to his own devices, a shirt would go on over a jumper and pants would be put on over pyjama bottoms. At bedtime he would think there was nothing wrong in going to bed in his daytime clothes.

We were back in the house for 10pm. Eddie took some

convincing it was bedtime and that night we were up and down the yard by torchlight at 11pm, looking for the cows. I eventually settled him around midnight.

At 1.30am he was off to the bathroom, both him and the bed soaking as he'd managed to pull the waterproof out of the bed. 'The roof must be leaking,' he announced. 'It's got all over me and the bed.'

I assured him we'd get someone to see to the roof in the morning and changed both him and the bed. That night the procedure was repeated at both 3.30am and 5.30am and I only managed about two hours sleep. I don't know which was worse: struggling with wet bed linen in the middle of the night, or tossing round fretting in bed in between disturbances.

I'm in the church choir but I didn't feel much like singing that Sunday morning. Eddie had woken around 6.30am, sure that he was expecting a delivery of straw and must be up. I just dragged around, feeling like my head was submerged in a bag, more robot than woman. He'd forgotten about 'the delivery' after breakfast and was content jobbing around in his workshop, with no repeat of the earlier confusion. Since I was up and sort of awake by now, I took myself off to the church service.

At this stage of the journey, because Eddie's confusion came and went, I did sometimes gamble during the day that all would be well and left him for short intervals. I always worried when I was away, wondering if I should have gone, and I breathed a sigh of relief when I returned to find him still pottering around the farm or in the house.

Once in church, my mind felt like a spinning cauldron of chaos but I tried to appear normal, to gather some peace within the ancient walls. The service made little impression; I do remember fighting tears during one of the hymns, mouthing the words rather than singing.

It was family-service day and the choir were sitting a few rows from the front with the congregation. As the uncontrollable welter of distress swept over me, a comforting hand slid over mine. This was to be another feature of this journey: the kindness and support I received from so many people.

After the service there were refreshments. I'd just about gathered myself together. I wanted to slip away but was persuaded to stay for a cup of tea.

'How's Eddie?' asked another friend. Fatal! The floodgates reopened.

I cried a lot during this journey; I suppose it was my way of releasing some of the pent-up emotion. I was like a pipe straining at a valve, the impending tears bubbling in the background. Every so often they had to burst out. If I hadn't released them, I felt as if I might explode with grief. I found tears would spring up at the least provocation. An unguarded word from someone, an impatient shop assistant, even trying to sort out routine bills and I'd find myself welling up. At times it felt as if I were forever on the edge of crying, which could result in wet eyes or a full-on wail. I tried not to cry in front of Eddie whenever possible.

Monday morning the phone rang; it was the neurologist's secretary. They'd received the letter and the specialist would see Eddie the next day at 9am. Don't knock the NHS; I know it's got problems but it's amazing when it works well. I registered both surprise at its efficiency and the hope that I'd manage to get Eddie to the city hospital by 9am. It was a good hour's drive away,.

'We'll have to get up early tomorrow,' I told Eddie that evening. 'We're going to hospital for you to see a special doctor.'

'Why?' he asked.

'They're just a bit worried about your head.'

He looked at me sadly. 'Am I going to die?'

I swallowed. 'Of course not, love, it's nothing like that. They just want to check on your eyesight.'

'Aye, it's not been so good recently. We need a better light in here.'

'I'll get a brighter bulb,' I assured him.

'The lighting's never been right since they mucked about with the wattage. These new-fangled bulbs hardly give out any light. I need brighter ones down in the cowshed, it's getting really difficult to milk.'

'We'll have a look round the shops, see if we can get some hundred-watt bulbs.'

I somehow managed to get him up at 6.30am the next morning. He was having one of his sleepy mornings after getting up five times during the night. He told me I was a pest.

It always took time these days to get him sorted. I'd pop down and boil a kettle, while he splashed around having a bit of a wash. He could still just about shave himself. He'd long scorned an electric razor, not using the one I'd bought him, and reverted back to his wet shave: 'Always feel like I've had a proper shave with a razor,' he'd say.

We left around 7.45, giving us just under an hour for the drive and fifteen minutes to get parked and find our way to the right clinic. Another increasing problem was Eddie's ability to walk. Days varied but thankfully this was a 'good leg day'. Taking our time, we reached the clinic reception with five minutes to spare.

It wasn't long before Eddie was called in to see the specialist. He was a middle-aged man with a quiet voice and sympathetic manner. Because of his soft tones Eddie heard little but, as he always said, 'I know you'll tell me what he was on about afterwards.'

He showed us the results of Eddie's brain scan, which had been carried out a few weeks earlier. 'See, this is the optic chiasma,' he said, pointing. 'That's where the optic nerves cross over before travelling back through the brain. It's a large berry aneurysm and it's pressing on both optic nerves. He might have had it for many years but it's just starting to cause problems.'

I looked at the scan, searching back over forty years to my nursing anatomy lessons, trying to keep calm and take in the information. 'You can also see the vascular damage to both hemispheres of the brain.' Again he pointed. 'It's very widespread.' I followed his finger, noting the masses of blank areas throughout the brain. Some were mere pin-pricks, others the size of a fingernail. 'These are the places where the brain has already died,' he said. 'As you can see, it's extensive.'

'What can be done?' I asked.

'Well, as you already know there's nothing can be done about the dementia. As to the aneurysm, that's not really up to me. He'll need a further referral to Newcastle. They can do a specialised procedure where they feed a line through blood vessels to the point of the aneurysm and the blood is drained away. As you'll understand, such an operation carries risk and it's debatable whether it's either advisable or practical with your husband's dementia and age.'

'What happens if he doesn't have the operation?'

'That depends on the aneurysm. If it stays the same size, he'll just continue with the reduced eyesight.' He didn't add the alternative, I could work that out for myself. 'Anyway, what I'll do now is bundle everything up and send it off to Professor .... You'll receive an appointment to go over and see him and he'll decide. While you're here, we'll take some bloods, and I'm going to send Mr Huck down to see our specialist ophthalmologist.'

I thanked him and we left the surgery. 'What's he say?' asked Eddie.

'You're going to have some bloods taken and see another eye doctor.'

'I'll be like a pin cushion. I hope the next chap speaks louder – I couldn't make out a word the last chap said.'

As we waited for the blood to be taken, I gave his hearing aids a check but they were both working okay. I knew it depended on how clearly and loudly someone spoke, and I realised that Eddie understood people he knew far better than strangers.

Half an hour later we were sitting outside the ophthalmology surgery. This really was the NHS at its best: caring and efficient. The neurologist had phoned the ophthalmologist and, with no wait or extra appointment, Eddie had been fitted in straight away. The nurse who'd brought us down handed in all Eddie's results and notes to the reception and Eddie was seen with no further preamble.

As I was to find on many future occasions, it was here that the double problem of Eddie's deafness and dementia would cause problems. The ophthalmic specialist was very nice but spoke with a strong Indian accent. Firstly Eddie couldn't hear him; secondly, he couldn't understand the instructions he was given. After struggling with the initial eye inspection, Eddie had to go into a special booth. The idea was that a light would be flashed in various places across his field of vision. Each time he saw a light, he had to press a button; this would determine what he could see.

I had to sit outside while all this was going on. I could hear instructions being repeated over and over. 'Just press the button when you see a flash of light, Mr Huck.' Silence. 'Did you see a light? No, don't keep your thumb on the button, just press when you see a light.' It went on for quite a while as I waited, knowing Eddie hadn't a clue what was going on. Perhaps he would have understood if they'd let me give him the instructions in a voice he was accustomed to.

Some while later it was over. Eddie came out of the booth, laughing. 'I don't know what the hell they wanted,' he said. 'I just kept pressing this damn button and they got all worked up.'

The ophthalmologist conceded that it had been difficult to carry out the tests. 'I think his peripheral vision is impaired,' he said. 'But he does have fairly good forward vision, enough to manage. I'll add my findings to the other details that are going to Newcastle. You should hear fairly soon about an appointment.'

Home we went and life carried on very much as it had before. My middle name was becoming 'Worry', and I found I was mulling the problem over and over, wondering what was going to happen. If it was left alone, Eddie's sight might remain the same or deteriorate, leaving him blind. If he had an operation, it could burst the aneurysm or cause some other side-effect, or it might solve the problem. But – and here I came up with my gigantic BUT – how could Eddie possibly cope in a strange hospital environment? He would not understand what was going on, would most likely be afraid and unable to hear what was said or to do what was asked of him.

Since the diagnosis of dementia I'd become a mother hen shepherding her chick, yet trying to let him carry on with his normal life as much as possible. The prospect of him being alone and troubled, having some dangerous and complicated operation without me there to hold his hand, filled me with dread.

Friday 25th February was an awful night. Eddie got up at 1.15, 2.30, 4.30, 5.15, 6.30 and 7.30am. I found myself standing sobbing in the bathroom at 4.30am. I eventually got up at 8.15 feeling dreadful, not helped by the electricity being off all day and continuous rain. The clouds outside mirrored my mindset: gloomy and grey.

The one bright event of the day was the arrival of the district nurse, who brought some incontinence pads. I'd asked the surgery who to phone a few days before. There were pads and string pants for Eddie to wear at night, but at the moment he was still dry during the day.

It's strange but that's how I came to live in Cumbria, as a district nurse; in some ways it was the completion of a circle. The nurse who came was nice but, apart from advice and handing over the pads, that seemed to be the limit of her involvement. It was so different when I was nursing. Then, if a patient like Eddie had been referred, I would have visited regularly, giving increasing care as was needed. As he became more disabled, I would have come with my nursing aide to give weekly baths. As the disease progressed, we might have been needed to get the patient up and dressed, with daily or twice-daily visits to give nursing care and support to the family. Now if this work is needed it is carried out by unqualified care assistants. I truly never understand the home role of a modern-day district nurse.

At this time Judy, a retired nursing friend, advised me to get some absorbent, machine-washable, waterproof bed pads. These were similar to the old draw-sheets, going across the bed under the patient and tucked in each side. When I was nursing, these sheets would have been on top of a narrow mackintosh, which again would have tucked under the mattress. The new bed pads were easy to find on the internet and I invested in four. They arrived a few days later and made bed protection much better.

Looking back on my few notes from this period, there seemed little to report for the next few days, apart from the arrival of the occupational therapist on 7th March – a Sunday! If I remember correctly, we were referred to him by the district nurse as I'd mentioned Eddie's increasing problems with walking and climbing stairs. I was to discover, as time progressed, that there's a lot of help out there once you're pointed in the right direction.

The OT suggested three things: a walking stick; a low bath seat, and two hand rails to help Eddie up the staircase. The stick would give some support and help to steady him when he was walking; the bath seat would make getting in and out better, and hopefully Eddie would get up the stairs easier by holding onto the extra rails.

He was asked to stand up and some measurements were taken. The OT brought a stick and cut it to size.

'I'll look a proper Charlie walking down the village using this,' laughed Eddie.

'The stick leads,' advised the therapist. 'Not too far ahead, then walk into it using the stick for balance.' By now we were outside the house as it was a fine day, Eddie holding the stick like it was his mucking-out brush.

'Stick, one, two,' urged the OT, as Eddie aimed the stick a good three feet in front of him. 'No, that's too far, just a short stride away.' This time stick and right leg moved in unison, like a stiff robot.

'It's harder than it looks,' Eddie observed as the therapist steadied him. The stick had now managed to lodge up between his legs.

'You'll get it with practice. You most likely won't need it indoors but it should help outside. I'll put in a request for your handrails,' he added. 'You'll get a letter.' He gave me a prescription for the bath seat and left shortly afterwards, Eddie happily waving the stick above his head like a flag.

From then on, we had walking trips down the back of the village whenever the weather was fine. 'I want to get back to walking properly,' said Eddie, as we headed out. I became like a drill sergeant: 'Stick, one, two,' I'd say over and over. Sometimes the drill was successful and we'd manage a good few yards before either turning into a robot walk or getting tangled. Sometimes we'd manage only a step or two, then Eddie would be ahead and the stick trailing somewhere behind.

'I'm Jake the Peg – diddle-iddle-iddle-um – with my extra leg,' we'd sing, as we laughed our way around the village.

In the next few weeks, the staircase rails were fitted and took the worry out of stair climbing for the time being. Eddie's hands were still strong and he could now pull himself upstairs on days when his legs felt wobbly.

I got the bath seat from the chemist and positioned it in the bath whenever Eddie went in. 'I don't like this damn thing,' he said, the first time he sat on it. The seat raised him about eight inches from the bottom of the bath, so most of his body sat above the water. This was a chap who for years had been a 'bath lounger'. Eddie often went to sleep in the bath, soothed and relaxed by the warm caress of the water. Now he seemed to perch above it like an ungainly duck. His knees stuck out, plus he must now balance as there was no back rest.

Some months before, we'd bought a non-slip bath mat and had two hand supports fitted to the tiles on one side of the bath. The first time Eddie used the bath seat, he slid forward and plopped with a big splash into the bottom of the bath. 'We'll wash the floor while we're at it,' he joked, as the cascade of water drenched the bathroom and me. I put a towel on it the next time, which helped, but I had to sit on the side of the bath behind him, propping him up to prevent him falling backwards. His muscles were gradually becoming weaker and sitting unsupported was impossible. Sadly, his 'lounging' days were over. Since it was quite an ordeal holding onto him, bath time was not a prolonged affair, but for the time being we managed.

March progressed with no word from Newcastle. It is impossible to worry all the time: 'what will be, will be.' I didn't think Eddie's sight was getting any worse as he still enjoyed watching his favourite programmes on the television and also worked his way through the paper every day. Outside, on good days when there was little confusion, he went back and forward to his workshop and I was able to leave him alone for a short time, with regular checks to make sure he was okay.

As the months progressed I learned that the chronic lack of sleep suffered by carers is perhaps the worse aspect. The body learns to cope and on the surface I appeared to be functioning normally. I didn't walk round yawning and only occasionally fell asleep during day. The exhaustion builds up gradually; in my case it was with a low-lying headache in the morning, at times an inability to think, and difficulty concentrating. Small tasks became mountains: just making out a shopping list, or looking for a phone number. I was still secretary of our WI and I'd written minutes for years with little thought; now I tried to gather words which slipped away. I would hunt in my mind for a phrase or name, becoming more and more frustrated.

The 7th March was a 'red-letter day' on The Journey; it was the day that the psychiatric nurse made her first visit. I'll call her Nurse Maggie. Her visit opened up all the other avenues of care; she shone a light into what services and help were available, but this was only a small part of her value. From that day onwards, I didn't feel quite as alone. She was not just an understanding, considerate ear to bend, she became a generous-hearted friend.

I remember being pretty controlled during her visit. We'd had a fairly good night, for a change. I told Nurse Maggie about Eddie and how things were progressing, and she talked to him, gently probing to see how he responded. Eddie was his usual happy self, chatting on to her mainly about the farm.

I told her the help we'd already received, including incontinence pads and OT aids.

'What about financial?' she asked. I'd honestly never thought about that. I suppose, compared to many people in similar circumstances, we were comfortable; we had some savings and both of us received pensions.

'You'll have extra expenses,' Maggie stressed. 'Washing clothes and bedding, travelling to appointments. You're entitled to a reduction in your Council Tax. If a member of your family is suffering from dementia, you receive a 25% discount.' That was news to me. 'Also, you're entitled to Attendance Allowance, in your case most likely the higher amount taking into consideration the night care. I'll get someone from Age Concern to come and help you fill in the forms and I'll inform the Council. They'll contact you.'

I now felt guilty. I suppose I'm from that age group; I didn't expect money to look after Eddie. Extra expenses were absorbed and we were not struggling.

'You're saving the government money by looking after your husband,' Maggie explained, brushing aside my objections. 'And you don't know what expenses you might incur for carers or additional help as the disease progresses. You're doing really well,' she assured me.

When she left, I had a phone number to contact if anything cropped up that I couldn't deal with, or if I was worried about something. I had a name, a real-life, breathing, professional person to whom I could speak in an emergency. I had a date on the calendar for her next visit but she'd come sooner if I needed her. Only someone who has been in this situation can imagine the relief that I felt.

The reason for the nurse's visit was lost on Eddie; he said she was 'a grand lass' but rapidly forgot she'd been. That afternoon we had a number of trips up and down the yard looking for the cows, Eddie only content when we'd been into every outbuilding. He scratched his head as he hunted through the cowshed. 'Well, I fed them earlier,' he said.

March slipped away with little change to our chaotic lifestyle and we heard nothing from Newcastle. Referring to my notes, there seemed little out of the ordinary to report until 1st April, when I made the following remarks.

***

April Fool's Day, well-named!

Today we took a step deeper into the unknown. My life is gradually dividing into two halves. In one way I try to cling onto normality. Today I went to the shop, visited a friend and had a sweet girl from the BBC's John Bishop's Britain come to interview me. (I'd become involved with the programme a few months before, after picking up a 'travelling email.' I think at this time any diversion from reality was welcome, and I ended up appearing on the show!) Then the second half of my life takes over, and there's been a lot of the second half today, even more than normal.

Eddie is convinced there are other people in the house. He's spent much of the day telling them to go and asking me who they are. He was watching television when some sheep got into our front garden, real not imaginary. They were easily removed, but a short while later Eddie was off looking for a helicopter. 'It's herding the sheep round the garden,' he said, eyes scanning the sky.

I got him back indoors and made afternoon tea. 'Did you enjoy being in the helicopter?' he asked, then he started to laugh. 'Half the village was out watching you. I bet it's on Border News tonight.'

We'd barely finished tea when Eddie was pulling on coat and Wellingtons. 'Where you going?' I asked.

'I'll just go and give those cows some hay. They've been giving mouth, they must be hungry.' So off we went down to the cowshed. 'You don't need to come, I won't be long,' he said, but I went along as he wobbled off down the yard. He only used his stick when I reminded him; we'd already lost it about ten times and found it hanging on the back of doors, lying on walls and once in the wood pile.

Into the dark, empty cowshed, tumbling over stored gates and falling over stored, worn-out carpets. 'The cows were here this morning,' he insisted.

Back in the house, he settled for a short while. From 7pm he had no concept of where he was. He kept putting on his coat and the Wellies. 'We've got to be away home,' he demanded, heading out for the tenth time or more.

'We're at The Mill, we are home,' I insisted.

'No we're not! And where's our Ruby?'

'She's not here, she's at her own home.'

'She must be upstairs with all those people.' Off upstairs, in and out of bedrooms, back downstairs, coat and Wellies on and off. This never stopped until 10pm, when I convinced him it was bedtime.

'But where am I going to sleep?' he asked, puzzled.

I undressed him, and led him into our bedroom, hoping he was exhausted after all the activity. 'I'll never sleep in a strange bed. I'll lie awake all night and worry where I am,' he said.

I hope he doesn't.

***

A representative from Age Concern arrived on Wednesday 6th April. She was very helpful; thank goodness she understood the forms. I wonder how many elderly people miss out on financial and other help merely because the forms are too complicated? They call them forms but they're like small booklets and can be daunting.

She asked questions and knew where to put the relevant information. 'I'm almost sure you'll qualify for the higher level of Attendance Allowance, considering the number of hours you care for your husband during the day and the night,' she said.

I still couldn't help feeling guilty and pondered on what to spend the money on. 'It's awarded to Mr Huck,' she said. 'You can spend it on whatever you need. It can be anything that helps your situation.'

Looking back, I suppose we'd already had quite a few extra expenses. There were all the bed-protection things. I was washing Eddie's clothing and some bedding nearly every day, plus we'd paid out to have the grip handles attached to the bath tiles, and for the bath mat. At that time the bathroom was carpeted but I found that Eddie had been 'missing' the loo. It became necessary to take up the carpet and fit washable linoleum. As the months passed, I also needed to employ people to do jobs that Eddie had always undertaken; with hindsight, I suppose that the money was helpful. Anyone in the same position should remember that you are entitled to this money, and you can see from these examples that there are many ways it can be used.

Nurse Maggie arrived for her second visit on 14th. I gave her an update on what had been happening. We'd heard from the Council about the reduction in Council Tax and I told her Age Concern were sending off the forms. She had a good chat with Eddie over tea. She tried to convince him that he didn't need to worry about cows but, like me, she didn't get very far. She suggested a referral to a physiotherapist to see if Eddie's walking could be improved. Other than that, we agreed that I was coping for the moment, though life was difficult. As long as things got no worse, she would come again in June. She assured me that she, or one of her colleagues, was only a phone call away and not to hesitate to contact her if needed.

The last week in April an appointment arrived for Eddie to see a professor at Newcastle on 10th May about his aneurysm. I'd reached the point where I didn't know whether to be relieved that we were now going to get some decisions and possible action, or terrified at what might happen. We had a friend in the village who used to live in Newcastle and was quite happy to drive us, so that took the heat off me struggling through the one-way system on unknown territory.

While I continued to worry, the country rejoiced in the royal wedding of Prince William and Catherine on 29th April, which also happened to be our thirty-fifth wedding anniversary. It sort of crept up because I'd had so much on my mind. Eddie was having a few good days and went down to the shop to buy me a card and some flowers. He wanted us to go out for a meal but the places I fancied were all booked up with it being a special holiday. We did find somewhere which was passable and we had a good evening but, looking back, I wish we'd managed to go somewhere really special. It wasn't to be.

We made up for the disappointment by attending a wedding the next day. It was Arty and Marion's youngest daughter, Anna. It was a perfect service and she looked beautiful and happy. We went to the meal and dance in the evening and it was a truly memorable night. Eddie really enjoyed himself and, as often happened at this stage of the journey, he was fine apart from being a little wobbly on his legs. This uncertainty was the cruellest aspect of the situation: one day few problems, the next a quagmire of confusion.

Tuesday 10th May came and we were up early after one of our usual disturbed nights. Eddie wasn't sure why we were going to Newcastle, though I'd tried to explain, but he enjoyed the drive. Our friend, Joy, dropped us off outside the Royal Victoria Infirmary, and we headed inside to find the department of neurosurgery. It's a huge hospital, quite overpowering. Our local hospital and the Lancashire hospital where I'd trained seemed tiny in comparison. We were there in good time and had a cup of tea and a cake before going into the waiting room.

Eddie was smiling and cheerful, wondering what all the bother was about. I was calm on the outside but the opposite within. What if the professor wanted to operate? Would it be better to leave well enough alone? What if Eddie's eyesight got worse? Oh God! What if he went blind? I was approaching panic when Eddie's name was called. Hoping I wasn't going to deposit my tea and cake on the important professor's shoes, I entered his consulting room.

The only way I can describe him is 'a real gentleman'. He was accompanied by his registrar and they'd obviously been discussing Eddie's case before they met him. They didn't dither around looking up notes or consulting scans, they knew exactly what they were going to advise.

The professor was a handsome, middle-aged man, with a clear, polished voice; he radiated an air of knowledgeable ability. This was the legendary 'brain surgeon' from the well-known quip: 'What do you think you are? A brain surgeon.' This chap was the real deal. How does someone get to be that clever, that talented? Hard work, experience and dedication. This man had it in spades. 'Your life in his hands' – yes, I would have trusted this man with Eddie's or my own life. He had an understated magnificence; he was special.

He spoke to us both but I understood it was me he was mainly addressing. 'We've had a good look at all the information and my recommendation is that, for the time being, we do nothing,' he said. Did I give a sigh of relief?

'You're not seeing much either side of your field of vision, Mr Huck,' he continued. 'A bit like David and Goliath.' He laughed as I looked puzzled. 'I've always believed that's how David killed Goliath with his sling shot. Goliath had no peripheral vision and David sneaked up from the side. I'll be writing to your doctor and I'll recommend an eye test in another year. Should things become worse, we'll have another look at it and possibly consider intervention but, in view of the dementia,' he smiled at me, 'I think that's the best advice at the moment. Is that alright?'

I think he knew I was relieved. We shook hands. He said how good it had been to meet us, we thanked him and it was all over in just a few minutes.

And basically, that was that. I had to understand that the aneurysm would be left alone because of Eddie's age and dementia. Should his vision get worse, they could try to do something, but… And these were the unsaid words, the elephant in the room. It had been there when we'd seen the neurologist; it was there again when we saw the professor. The dementia might kill Eddie long before the aneurysm sent him blind.

CHAPTER 4

CLINGING ON

I've called this chapter 'Clinging On', but perhaps I should have called it the jumble sale! Imagine a heap of clothing piled on a table. You start to delve in, pulling items to the top. Anything can come up from a pea-green size twenty-four skirt to a bikini. The items are tossed around as you search through to the bottom. More stuff emerges until jumpers and shirts are flying around in all directions, some hitting the floor. Amongst it might be found a piece of treasure, a blouse that's just the right size and goes with that pair of pants, but most of it is no use. Junk.

Over the next few months this is what happened to Eddie's mind. There were still good days and these were the pieces of treasure, but so often the junk took control. I made few notes as I had neither the energy nor inclination to write more. This has made that period the most difficult to recall as I have to dredge back through my memories. The time scale is a blur; I remember events and major incidents but in what order they occurred is lost. Perhaps part of my brain doesn't want to remember.

Forgive me, then, if the next part of our journey sounds disjointed. Others who tread this path will find the same problems; my only advice is to keep going as best you can and try to keep your emotions under control.

It was also as this period progressed that I changed tack in my approach to dementia. I was given a book which followed the progression of dementia patients as they advanced into the disease. The most important piece of advice I received is not to question or correct the patient but accept what they say whenever possible.

***

May slipped away. It rained a lot; it was a notoriously wet summer. What do I remember?

The expansion of the second stage of our journey. In the early days Eddie's confusion was mainly confined to the approach of darkness and night, with little blips during the day; now the confusion became established. Each day we faced the unknown, and anything could happen. It meant that it was increasingly difficult to leave him alone for any length of time. A quick pop to the shop was possible, but if I went anywhere for a few hours either someone had to keep an eye out for him or he must come with me.

John was a godsend. He understood the problem and frequently now he and Eddie would be busy with jobs for a few hours, which meant I could slip away. He made allowances for Eddie's increasing inability to walk any distance, sitting him down in the old cowshed while he worked. To Eddie's great hilarity, John provided Eddie with a 'throne' on the trailer. When they were working up the fields, John would drive the tractor trailing Eddie behind, up on his seat.

John still tells the tale of 'the cup of tea'. He was busy down in the shed, Eddie 'helping' while they chatted.

'Do you want a cup of tea?' Eddie asked.

'Okay, that'll be fine,' said John.

So away Eddie went, up to the house to make a drink. He was gone for ages; John was starting to get worried and was just about ready to go looking for him. Suddenly Eddie arrived, dishevelled, hair all over the place, bits of vegetation stuck in his jumper.

'Where've you been, Eddie?' asked John.

'Well, I don't rightly know but it was a long way.' The cup was only a quarter full, the majority of the contents having spilled on the return journey, and it was cold. We worked out he must have come out of the side door of the house but, instead of turning right to walk back down the yard, he turned the other way. We presume he ploughed his way through the deep undergrowth behind the house where it's like a jungle, especially in spring and summer. He must have lost himself in the tangle, only eventually finding his way back to the old cowshed where they were working. John still has a laugh when he remembers Eddie arriving back, clutching the remains of the cup of tea.

Nights were unchanged and I'd got into the habit of totting up how much sleep I'd managed. 'Up at 12 midnight, back to bed 12.10. Fell asleep around 12.30, up 1.30am. Tossed until about 2am, up 2.45. Fell asleep somewhere after 3.30, up 4.30. Managed at get back to sleep fairly quickly, but up again 5.30. Tossed until 6.15, up 7.30. Eddie awake, so got up. Number of hours around three and a half.' This may sound obsessive, but I wondered how long I could keep going on this 'chopped-up' sleep and I decided to ask the doctor if anything could be done. I didn't want Eddie to be drugged but was the 'toilet trot' just the dementia or was it a bladder problem?

I sent in a sample of urine and we made an appointment to see our GP. At this stage there was no infection but the doctor said Eddie's prostate was a bit enlarged; he'd try some pills. The aim of the medication was to lower Eddie's need to pass water during the night and this, hopefully, would mean we would both sleep better.

The effect was miraculous; just two days into the course Eddie only got up once during the night. For the first time in months we managed three, four or even five hours' unbroken sleep. It was wonderful. This utopia lasted for just over a week.

It had been a difficult few days. We'd spent many hours up and down the yard in all weathers searching for cows. Again the house was filled with people and Eddie was afraid to go upstairs in case they grabbed him. He'd been in and out of bed during the day as morning became night and an hour stretched to a day.

One evening I'd laid the table for the evening meal and Eddie was unusually quiet as we sat down to eat. He always had a good appetite and would eat anything; he was never a 'picky' man. He took a few mouthfuls, pushed his plate away and rushed to the sink, spitting out food. He also emptied his handkerchief, where he'd secreted part of his meal, into the kitchen bin.

A stranger looked at me as he turned from the sink, leering. 'I know what you're up to,' he said.

'What's the matter?' I asked.

'I know. You can't fool me. You want to poison me.'

'No, Eddie, that's stupid. Sit down and eat the rest of your meal.'

'Not likely, you just want me out of the way.'

'Eddie, you know I'd never hurt you.'

This was greeted by a sly laugh and nodding of his head as he curled into an armchair. 'I know. It's alright, I know. I heard you talking to them.'

'Talking to who?'

More soulless laughter. 'Upstairs. I heard you. You can't kid me.'

'Honestly, Eddie, it's all in your mind.' By now I was starting to get upset and trembling.

'I know what you're up to, Jackie. You think I'm a fool but I'm not.'

I think I was sobbing by this time. He turned away, absorbed in the television. Silence descended between us and, not for the first or last time, I didn't know what to do or say.

It was nearly midnight when he agreed to go to bed. He made me walk ahead, not trusting me to be behind him. He struggled to get undressed alone, pushing me away. I think he was exhausted when he fell asleep. I know I was.

We both slept well, Eddie only getting up once. He seemed to have calmed and whatever had triggered the suspicions had gone. I phoned Nurse Maggie after breakfast, and told her what had happened. 'Anything different this last week?' she asked.

'Only the pills for his waterworks. We've had such good nights.'

'It's the pills, they can have this affect. Stop them and contact your doctor. I'll be away for a few days. If you need an urgent visit, contact the office and one of my colleagues will come.'

I told the doctor, who agreed it was the pills. 'They can cause confusion,' he said, 'but it was worth trying.' I couldn't help but think he might have warned me.

It took two days for the pills to wear off. Eddie was still confused but didn't turn on me again. The third night we were up eight times – back to 'normal'.

***

Somehow we carried on, trying to keep life as normal

as possible when we could. I did a couple of speaking engagements and took Eddie with me. He was fine, apart from thinking he must pay for the proffered cup of tea. We had an official launch for my book at the market hall, my first published work, Cats Like Me – well, it had to be about cats, didn't it? It was a wonderful, memorable evening. More than eighty people turned up and, as I sat signing copies, it was a dream come true.

We went to a funeral and into town. It was the annual church exhibition, which I helped set up, and we had a trip over to see Ruby. We also went over to the outskirts of Blackpool to film my bit in John Bishop's Britain. There was only the film crew and director present. The village hall caretaker and Eddie were the audience; he was captivated by it all and we had a lovely day.

We were sitting in the garden during a rare sunny afternoon when Eddie turned to me. 'Where are they?' he asked.

'Where are what?'

'The rabbits,' he said.

I'd just finished reading the book about dementia, so was now trying out the suggestions. 'We have some rabbits?'

'Yes, the ones we bought this morning at Kirkby Stephen. We brought them home in the back of the car. Are they still there?'

'Oh, those rabbits. They must be up in the top barn.'

'We'll have to get them a hutch,' he said. 'We'll go and buy them one tomorrow.'

'Good idea. Perhaps you'd prefer to make a hutch.'

'I should have some wood down in the shed. Let's go and look.' We walked down to the shed, pausing by the garden wall as Eddie's legs weren't good that day.

'Our Bobby was here earlier.'

'Oh, how is he?' I asked.

'Fine, he's always busy. He has too much to do.'

'Did he have Mary with him?' Mary was Bobby's wife.

'No, she'd gone to see our Ruby.' He leaned against the wall, taking in the sun, watching swallows flying above. 'Where were we going?'

'Just having a little walk, love. Do you want to go back in the garden?'

'Aye, I think all that walking I did yesterday must have tired me.' We went back to the garden, and I made us afternoon tea on the lawn. No mention was made of rabbits again.

I became used to unreal conversations. Here's a sample, one of the few notes I jotted down at the time. My resolve to 'agree with everything' failed on this occasion.

Eddie: 'There's a lady coming Friday afternoon, she'll be coming to the bungalow.'

Me: 'Which bungalow?'

Eddie: 'Well, she'll be seeing the old lady.'

Me: 'What old lady?'

Eddie: 'John Porter's sister.'

Me: 'She's dead.'

Eddie: 'So they'll go by train to the bungalow?'

Me: 'Who?'

Eddie: 'Those two chaps.'

Me: 'What two chaps?'

Eddie (shaking his head): 'The ones who came today with all that stuff down in the cowshed.'

Me: 'No one's been today with anything.'

Eddie: 'Well, it'll be a big morning tomorrow, sorting it all out.'

Me: 'Sorting what out?'

Eddie: 'All that stuff?'

Me: 'There's no stuff.'

Eddie: 'So, it's down at the bungalow?'

Me (completely lost the thread at this point): 'Yes, that's where it is.'

Eddie: 'So this woman's coming in the morning.'

Me: 'No one's coming tomorrow.'

Eddie: She's going to see that old girl at the bungalow?'

Me: 'Yes, that's right.'

I remember one evening Eddie had been up and down to bed a number of times, but eventually settled. I always popped upstairs during these times to make sure he was okay. Sometimes I would hear him bumping about and I'd go and check what he was up to. This night I went upstairs and, to my horror, there was no sign of him. I searched through every room in the house but he wasn't there. I put the outside light on and realised the back door was unlocked.

As I was pulling on a coat, he turned up, coming back up the yard. He was wearing a jacket over his pyjamas but nothing on his feet. 'Where ever have you been?' I said, trying not to sound as alarmed as I felt.

'Oh, I was just checking on the cows. There's one due to calf but it's hellish dark out here. I fell over,' he said, pulling off his jacket.

'You didn't hurt yourself?'

'No, I'm just a bit wet.' His pyjamas were damp as there was a fine drizzle coming down, and he was a bit muddy round the knees, plus his feet were cold and dirty. I got him back upstairs, washed and changed him, and settled him to sleep with a hot chocolate. From that day on, I hid the door keys.

Another similar up and down night, I'd checked on Eddie and found him asleep. I went up to bed a short while later but discovered I couldn't put the light on.

Eddie was only pretending to be asleep and was suddenly alert and out of bed. 'There was a fire,' he said, 'but I put it out.' He'd switched on the bedside lamp then emptied a full glass of water over the hot bulb, blowing up the lamp.

The physiotherapist arrived on 1st June. She came weekly for the next month, giving Eddie walking exercises, trying to make him take smaller steps and use his stick correctly. She was very good and patient but I couldn't help thinking she was wasting her time. Eddie not only rapidly forgot any instructions but soon didn't even remember she had visited.

Everywhere I went, we now went together; if I couldn't take Eddie, I didn't go. I did manage the odd trip somewhere when one of Eddie's cousins or a friend would come and stay with him for a few hours, and I still went to WI meetings each month as Arty came up to the house and kept Eddie company.

A gentleman from Eden Carers arrived on 17th June. He talked about the Alzheimer's Society and the services they offered to help carers cope. There was day care available, or alternatively a carer could come to the house, pick up Eddie and take him somewhere he might be interested in. 'Where do you think he'd like to go?' he asked.

'He likes animals. Somewhere he could see them.'

All this sounded good – but how would Eddie react to a stranger? Would he settle in a day-care centre? Even though I was now being offered some of the support I'd craved, I decided I could cope, at least for the present. The man gave me all the relevant information for when I felt such help was needed.

It was the middle of July when, in my own mind, I decided we had entered into the third phase of the dementia. We had started with evening confusion, which had progressed to additional day-time confusion; now psychotic intervals were added into the mix. We'd already had the little 'blip' when he'd thought I was poisoning him but that had been brought on by a reaction to the tablets. Now the psychosis became associated with the dementia, and was the most difficult and distressing of the symptoms. What made it worse was that I was the target of his delusions and there was no way I could talk him out of them. Anything I said, anything I did, made him worse. They rarely struck during the day but I began to dread the night.

An attack would come on without warning. Sometimes they struck after a bad day, where he'd been confused most of the time. Other times they came out of the blue after a day of relative calm.

One such event happened after a troubled afternoon and evening when he'd decided it was bedtime at 2pm. He'd been up again an hour later, then was up and down the stairs like a yo-yo until 7pm. I'd made an evening meal, which he reluctantly ate saying it was only an hour ago since he'd eaten, though I knew he'd had nothing since lunch.

'Right, I'm off,' he said, standing up.

'Where are you going?'

'Anywhere, as long as it's away from you.'

'But why, love? Sit down and watch the telly.'

'I know you've got that knife hidden. I'm going before you use it,' he said, heading into the hall.

'Don't be stupid,' I said, trying to pull him back into the house.

He shook me off, dashing to the back door, searching for the key which I'd hidden. 'Where's the key? Open this door, let me out!' he demanded, yanking the door handle up and down. Then he was pulling back on the handle, frantically trying to get the door open.

'No, Eddie, you're not going out.'

'I'll find a brick or a hammer and break this damn glass,' he said, turning away into the pantry where he kept his tools.

By now I was shaking, out of my depth, not knowing what I could do. If I remember correctly, at this point the phone rang. I answered it, crying. It was Mary, Bobby's widow from down south, asking how things were. I vaguely remember sobbing that I couldn't talk at the moment as Eddie was trying to break down the door. Goodness knows what she thought.

We were now struggling in the hall; thankfully he hadn't found the hammer, just an old shoe. He was using this as a weapon to bang against the glass in the door with one hand, while fending me off with the other. I was begging him to stop, doing everything I could think of to calm him, but nothing was working.

I decided I had no option but to open the door before he either broke the glass or hit me. It was debatable which would get a good clobbering first. Now we were off down the yard, Eddie running away from me as best he could on his wobbly legs, me tagging behind, pleading with him to stop.

I got ahead and talked him into stopping at the house of our nearest neighbours, just outside the yard. I knocked on the door and Joe answered. Sobbing, I asked him to talk to Eddie, to make him understand I wasn't going to hurt him.

We went inside their house. Joe had known Eddie most of his life and he managed to calm him. Then, as suddenly as the incident had blown up, it disappeared. Ten minutes later we were walking back to the house as if nothing had happened. We watched TV for a while, then Eddie went back to bed.

During these awful events I had to turn to friends; without them, I could not have managed. When Eddie was having one of these delusional episodes, he would usually calm down and listen to other people, as long as he knew them well. Four main people helped, Arty and Marion (what would I have done without them?), and Charlie and Nick, who own the bungalow across from The Mill. I forget how many times I frantically phoned one of these kind people, who dropped everything and rushed round to the house.

One night things were so bad, we had to send for the on-call doctor to give Eddie something to soothe him. Nick and Charlie were there that night and they'd been talking to him for an hour. They'd pacified him a little but he was still sure I was going to shoot him if they left. The doctor came and gave me two pills for him. I managed to grind them up and give them to him in some hot chocolate. They kicked in fairly quickly and Nick managed to get Eddie upstairs to bed before he went completely off his legs. He slept for twelve hours.

Was this the answer? Would I now have to resort to some form of emergency drug therapy? I consulted the doctor, who gave me some tablets. Fresh problems now reared their heads. When Eddie became so agitated, he would not take any medication. The only way to get anything down him was to slip it into a drink, usually hot chocolate, which he liked, but sometimes he'd even refuse the chocolate. If he did take the medication he became sluggish and slept, which was fine, but when he woke he was unable to stand.

He might sleep for about four hours then be awake wanting the toilet, but he couldn't walk to the bathroom. Sometimes he'd already soaked the bed, having dislodged the bed-protectors. Because of the medication he couldn't stand up, and he wouldn't roll back and forward while I changed sheets. I had an office chair on castors. I could just about manage to haul him onto that and push him into the bathroom. Here he'd struggle on and off the toilet, then I'd leave him on the chair while I changed the bed. This was all happening in the early hours of the morning and could happen twice or more in a night.

Nurse Maggie was bumping up her visits, first to monthly, then two weekly and finally to each week, with emergency calls in between. She advised a visit from the psychiatric consultant Eddie had seen at our local hospital in February. He arrived a few days later to reassess the situation. He was as kind and considerate as the first time, asking Eddie and me questions, nodding, taking notes. 'All the best, Eddie,' he said as he left.

I followed him to the door. 'Is there anything you can give him for the delusions?'

He smiled. 'We can try a very small dose of medication but I'm afraid even a tiny dose will most likely affect his mobility.'

'For how long do you think he'll still be able to walk?' I asked.

'I'd be very surprised if your husband is still on his feet in four months. He has a very severe form of dementia, which is advancing rapidly.'

'He already calls me by different names at times,' I said, trying to hold on to my composure. 'Will it get worse?'

He took my hand. 'In six months or less, your husband will not even recognise his own face in the mirror, let alone know you. The day will come when you'll have to start thinking about him going into care.'

I shook my head, the tears threatening. 'No, I'll be able to cope. He'll never have to go into care.'

He smiled as he left. 'You may have no choice,' he said kindly.

***

I was still holding occasional meetings at home; this allowed me to keep an eye on Eddie but still take part in something I enjoyed. The writers' group was one example; they were meeting monthly at The Mill but September was the last time.

The six of us, gathered in our sitting room. Eddie was in the living room. He'd had his evening meal and was watching television and poking through the paper. The meeting started at 7.30, and I slipped through to see him every fifteen minutes to make sure he was okay.

All was quiet for the first half hour then I heard footsteps passing the sitting room door. I popped out to see Eddie's back disappearing up the stairs. 'You off to bed?' I asked.

'No, I'm just going upstairs to see if those chaps have gone.'

'I'll come with you.' I shot back into my guests, told them I wouldn't be long, and followed Eddie upstairs. We searched through the bedrooms, ending up in the bathroom. 'I think they must have gone,' I said. Uncertainly he agreed and we went back downstairs. I again settled him in the living room. 'Do you want to come next door and sit with the writers' group?' I asked.

'No, I'm going to bed soon.'

I went back to my friends and assured them everything was under control. They knew about the problem and were understanding. Ten minutes later, we heard bumping and banging on the ceiling; Eddie had obviously crept back upstairs. I again excused myself and dashed away to find him in the bathroom. He'd put his pyjamas on over his clothes and was wandering around the upstairs landing.

'Are you ready for bed?' I asked.

'Of course,' he told me. 'It's past midnight.'

'Let's get you undressed properly,' I said, steering him

back into the bathroom. I got his clothes off, put on his pyjamas and led him to the bedroom.

'This isn't my room.'

'It is, love.' I turned the bed down and persuaded him to get in.

'They won't like me being in their room,' he stressed.

I stayed with him a while and he seemed to calm, then I slipped back downstairs to the writers.

I made cups of tea and coffee and gave out biscuits, but soon after I was back upstairs as we could hear more bumping and banging. This time when I reached our bedroom door I couldn't open it. I pushed, wondering what was going on. 'Eddie, are you alright?' I called.

'I'm keeping them out. They were trying to get in. They want to kill me.'

I had to heave to get the door open. When at last I gained entry, I discovered, that Eddie had taken everything out of the wardrobe and piled it up behind the door. My skirts, cardigans, jumpers and blouses were all messed up with Eddie's clothes as he'd worked to form a barricade. He was hiding, having pulled the sheets and blankets over his head.

The girls left early and I spent a long time trying to pacify Eddie. I gave him one of the emergency tablets ground up in hot chocolate, which sent him to sleep for a few hours. But when he awoke his bed was soaked as he'd pulled his pad off in his sleep, and he was unable to stand, So, we continued to whirl like a merry-go-round.

'We could ask for someone to come one or two nights a week. They could look after Eddie while you get some sleep,' said Nurse Maggie on one of her visits. Was this the answer, a carer looking after Eddie while I got some rest? I gave the idea thought, trying to take my own advice to not turn away help and give anything offered a chance, but a number of questions presented themselves.

Would I sleep? There was no guarantee. By now I was so tuned to wake at Eddie's slightest movement – could I just curl up in the spare room? How would Eddie react to a stranger in the house? What if he became convinced they were there to kill him? If he did accept them, his legs were becoming increasingly weak even without medication, especially in the middle of the night. Would they be able to get him to the bathroom time and again? Would he even go with them? The questions piled up; the doubt and worry gathered. Reluctantly, I refused the help. I was still coping – we could still cope.

On 22nd August we were visited for the first time by a social worker who had been appointed to our case. To me it seemed a bizarre situation that it was now deemed necessary for us to have a social worker. Help had been piling in over the past few months since Nurse Maggie had taken control; each person had helped to a greater or lesser degree.

Somehow, when Maggie said social worker it felt as if matters were about to slip out of my control. A nurse I could understand; I'd been a nurse and I felt at ease in her company. My dealings with social workers when I was nursing had been with problem families, uncared-for children, people in crisis or the desperate elderly. Social workers were an unknown quantity; they had power, could take command, make difficult and important decisions. It was, therefore, with a sense of trepidation that I welcomed her into the house.

She arrived with a smile and a handshake, introduced herself and was soon chatting to both Eddie and me. I will call her Rachel. She was tall and slender, a good-looking woman who knew her job and was good at it. She instilled an air of compassionate efficiency and soon allayed my fears. She assured us she was there to help and asked what I needed at that point in time to make caring for Eddie easier.

I explained that I was finding it increasingly difficult to go anywhere without him. Though I worried how he would react to someone he didn't know, it would help if I could have a few hours each week when someone could look after him while I went out. I said that relatives and friends had been very supportive but I didn't like to keep bothering people. I also told her that I was having to keep the doors locked to stop Eddie leaving the house without me knowing, and that I was anxious he could come to harm if he wandered off.

'Let's see what we can do,' she said, as she filled in forms and made notes. 'I'm sure Maggie has suggested day care. I really would encourage you to look at this again. The Alzheimer's Society run day care locally twice weekly, Monday and Thursday. Shall I ask the gentleman who organises it to come and see you?'

'Eddie doesn't have Alzheimer's, it's vascular dementia.'

'They care for people suffering from all forms of dementia.'

'A chap from Eden Carers suggested day care back in June but I wasn't keen. I'm not sure how Eddie will react,' I pondered as Eddie sat quietly. I never knew on these occasions how much he heard and, if he did hear, how much he understood. I always felt uneasy talking about him and making decisions about his life in front of him as if he weren't there. 'Well, perhaps once a week,' I mused. 'Each Thursday.'

Rachel's face lit up; she had the sort of face which could fill with joy. 'Why not go for the two days?' she said. 'That will give you a bit more time to yourself. You'll be able to get out and see friends besides doing some shopping. You'd enjoy a trip out in a taxi, wouldn't you, Eddie?' she asked, turning to him.

'As long as the wife comes as well,' he assured her.

'Don't worry, it will sort out. The Alzheimer's helpers are wonderful. He'll really enjoy himself and he'll have his lunch there each day.'

Reluctantly I agreed. Rachel said she'd phone the organiser, who would contact me to make a home appointment. 'Just so he and Eddie can have a chat,' she said. 'Now, what about getting some alarms fitted to the doors?'

She stayed an hour and left me her office and mobile number. 'I'll come again in six weeks,' she said. We agreed 4th October. 'By then, the day care will be up and running and we'll be able to see how things are going. If you need me before, don't hesitate to phone.'

'She was nice,' said Eddie after she'd gone. 'What was she on about?'

'She was sorting out a few days out for you.'

'Will you be coming?'

'No, this is something special for you. They'll come and pick you up in a taxi and bring you home. There'll be lots of things to do there and you'll have your lunch.'

'I don't want to go. I'd sooner stay here.'

'Well, we won't worry about it for now. It won't be for a few weeks.' And there it was left for the time being. Eddie rapidly forgot all about the conversation and I was left with new worries about how he would cope at a day centre.

Nurse Maggie arrived for her regular visit a few days later and was delighted I'd agreed to try day care. 'It will give you a break,' she said. 'And I'm sure you'll find that Eddie will settle.'

The 8th September was the Westmorland County Show. We went each year and Eddie loved it, especially the shire horses. I'd been pondering for a few weeks how to get him to the show this year, knowing how uncertain his mobility was. I'd contacted the show secretary and made us vice-presidents;

this meant we could park much nearer to the show ground. There were a number of member perks: transport from the parking ground up to the members' tent; free tea and coffee in the tent all day, and a special VIP seating area overlooking the main arena. I was also spending an hour in the WI tent selling and signing my book, and I made sure Eddie could sit with me.

The day went off well; only the weather didn't behave. We drove without problem into the special car park and were soon being ferried to the tent. I sorted us out with refreshments and we spent time in the members' enclosure watching the show. The WI tent was nearby and Eddie relished the bustle of people all around.

After another drink, we walked just a short way to watch the hounds and the huntsmen in their red coats preparing to gallop around the ring. Sadly, the rain was coming down and Eddie was feeling cold and tired. 'Do you want to go home?' I asked. He nodded and we took the buggy back to the parking lot. We'd only seen a small section of the show but he had managed to see a few horses and he'd enjoyed himself. It was the last time he ever went to the County Show. What a pity the sun didn't shine.

The gentleman from the Alzheimer's Society arrived the next day to sort out the day centre. He was a small, compact man with a foreign accent which Eddie couldn't understand, of course. He was very understanding and was sure that Eddie would settle without trouble. 'The taxi will come at 9.15am,' he said, 'and he'll be home around 3.15.' Eddie would start going on 26th September.

This agreed, he left – but I still couldn't feel comfortable with the arrangement. The more I thought about it, the more I worried. Was it just the 'mother-hen' protective attitude kicking in?

It was sometime around now that a regular new element was added to Eddie's confusion. It started any time from 6pm to 9pm. I began to dread the words: 'Well, let's away home.' These words spoken, Eddie would be out of his chair and into the hall, pulling on coat and Wellingtons. I'd stopped contradicting him as that could bring on a psychotic attack; also, when he started on this track nothing could distract him from his purpose.

I did try gentle persuasion. 'We're already home.'

'We don't live here,' he'd say. 'Come on, let's be off.'

So off we went. I'd grab coat, money and car keys and load Eddie into the car. Sometimes a quiet drive round the village would be sufficient. We'd come back up our lane and Eddie would happily wander in having 'come home'. At other times he was far harder to convince and he'd take control, directing me where to drive. On these occasions we could travel miles and be out for a few minutes or an hour.

Our village has four exits, so we had a wide choice of routes. Eddie would steer our expedition up and down narrow lanes, in and out of the nearby villages. We'd travel both B and A roads, venturing as far as nearby towns. We drove over moorland, passing farms, fields and isolated hamlets.

When he tired of his directing, I would try to take control and work our way back to the village. On one journey, about ten miles from The Mill, Eddie pointed down a narrow track. 'That's where I used to go on holiday. That's our Dan's place. I used to go for part of the summer, helping get the hay in. God! It were hard work but the grub was good.'

'It doesn't sound much like a holiday,' I said, laughing.

We went on sunny evenings and in driving rain, until eventually we would arrive 'home' and Eddie would be content, though occasionally we might have two excursions in an evening.

Wednesday 21st was my WI evening. I was still secretary, though I wasn't finding it easy. Arty arrived to sit with Eddie around 7pm and I slipped away. I had a good evening but I was starting to find social gatherings difficult because my state of mind was so fragile. We always begin our meetings singing 'Jerusalem'; now I found it impossible to sing without bubbling into tears. It's awful when you feel this great torrent struggling to escape; you swallow, blink, fumble with a file of papers, anything so you don't make eye contact with anyone or that's it! Gush!

I arrived home just after 10pm. It was obvious that Arty's evening hadn't been easy.

Eddie was sitting in his outdoor jacket and Wellingtons. He stood up as I walked in. 'About time,' he said. 'We've got to be away.'

'Where you going, Eddie?' asked Arty, before turning to me. 'He's been up and down all evening. That jacket's been on and off more times than I can count.'

'We've got to go home,' said Eddie, heading for the door.

I assured him we'd be off soon, thanked Arty and showed him out. I knew that it was becoming unfair to ask him to stay with Eddie for a full evening; there is only so much you can ask of friends. WI meetings, like everything else, were now impossible.

***

The morning of the 26th dawned. We'd had one of our usual disturbed nights. I got up at eight but Eddie took some persuading. 'You've got to get your breakfast and be ready for the taxi,' I told him as I managed to get him out of bed and into the bathroom.

'Are we going on holiday?' he asked as I washed and

dressed him.

'No, you're going for a little trip out. It's just for a few hours.'

'Are you coming?'

'No, not this time. It'll be a change for you and you can have a good crack.'

'I don't want to go,' he said as we headed downstairs. All my worst fears gathered.

He had breakfast and took his pills, and I got his shoes on just as the taxi was drawing up. I got him into his coat and we walked outside. Reluctantly he got into the taxi, his eyes never leaving mine. 'I am coming back?' he asked.

'Of course, love. It's just for a few hours while I do a bit of shopping.'

His eyes sparkled with tears but he tried to smile, that same loving, trusting smile. The taxi backed down the yard and I could see his face pressed against the car window, his hand waving, as they drove slowly away.

I went back into the house and collapsed in tears. I tried to think how Eddie must be feeling, abandoned amongst strangers, sent off somewhere he didn't want to go, not knowing where he was going. He must feel frightened and alone, betrayed by the one he loved and trusted the most. The more I remembered his face through that taxi window, the more I shook with uncontrollable weeping. I had to stop myself jumping in the car and rushing after the taxi to bring him home. It took me a long time to calm down.

I didn't go out that day; I just couldn't have faced anyone. I kept listening for the telephone, as they'd promised to ring if I was needed. I did soak in a relaxing bath, just letting the warmth soothe away the tension. Baths had been rushed for quite a while because I couldn't leave Eddie alone without worrying. I have no memory of the rest of the day; perhaps

I slept, perhaps I watched television. Physically I was at Mill House but mentally I was at day care, wondering how Eddie was coping.

I was relieved when the taxi returned around 3.15. Eddie clambered out and headed into the house. 'How did you get on?' I asked.

'I'm not going again,' he said, pulling off his coat. 'They're all crackers.'

'What do you mean?'

'Some chap was doing a jigsaw. This other one kept muttering. I don't know what he was on about. And some woman was singing. I'm not going there with a load of daft people!'

'Were the staff nice? What was the food like?' I asked, trying to find something positive from the experience.

'Oh, they were okay and we had pie and chips for dinner. That was good.'

'Well then, it wasn't all bad.'

'If it's so good, you go next time,' he said. 'I'm going to check on the cows.' With that, he was off down the yard.

The man came to fit the alarms the next day. We had them attached to both the back and front doors. I was shown how everything worked and warned that, once the alarm went off, I had just a few minutes to cancel it before the alarm would be raised back at the central headquarters. 'Someone will ring from the call centre,' the man said. 'They'll ask if everything is alright. If they don't get an answer, they'll try again and then send help.' It all sounded wonderful. Eddie would no longer be able to slip out without my noticing; I could now go upstairs knowing that if he left the house I would be alerted.

I was to find that there were drawbacks. Eddie would be sitting in the living room watching the television or resting.

I would make sure the alarm was on and go upstairs to the toilet or to do a job. Suddenly I would hear the shriek of the alarm telling me he'd left the house.

It was not always possible – or practical, with arthritic legs – to dash downstairs within a given time to cancel an alarm. Sometimes I made it, switched it off, then went in search of Eddie; sometimes I didn't. Soon after the phone would ring. A voice with a strong Liverpool accent would say, 'Are you alright, Edwin?' I would then have to assure her all was under control before rushing off to find him.

I had to remember to switch the alarm off when I was downstairs or it would start shrieking each time I opened the door. It also went into 'panic' mode if someone came to the door and I opened it, forgetting the alarm was still set. On numerous occasions over the next few months I jumped with shock at the sudden blaring of the siren. Eddie thought it was hilarious and was always opening the door out of sheer mischief just to set it off.

I was not looking forward to Thursday. Eddie had not mentioned the day care again and I had been reluctant to bring up the subject. On the Wednesday evening, I decided to broach the subject. 'I'm going shopping tomorrow,' I said, as we finished the evening meal.

'Where are we going?' he asked.

'Well, I'm going into town but there's a lot of walking, so you'd best not go.'

He nodded, quite happy with this explanation. 'I've got some jobs to do with the cows,' he said. 'They need fluking.'

I could feel my heart pounding. 'You'll be going to the day centre like last time. It's just for a few hours.'

'With that load of daft people?' he asked. He'd obviously not forgotten everything about that first day.

'They're not that bad and you liked the staff. You'll be

having your dinner there.'

'We'll see,' he said ominously.

Neither of us slept much that night, which was especially bad. He must have been up about ten times, and I had to change the bedclothes twice as he'd dislodged the protective coverings. He only really went into a deep sleep around 6am. I knew he must be up no later than eight for me to have time to get him washed, dressed and downstairs for breakfast.

After much encouragement, I eventually got him up about 8.30. I was beginning to wonder if it was worth the bother. He was ready just before the taxi was due. 'What's all the rush?' he asked.

'The taxi comes, at 9.15.'

'What taxi?'

Oh God! This was hard work. 'The taxi to take you to the day centre.'

'I don't want to go,' he said, starting to get angry.

'It's just for a few hours. I do need to go shopping. You won't be there long.' I could hear the taxi drawing up outside. Eddie dragged his feet as I managed to walk him through the door. The driver helped him in.

Should I say, 'Don't bother, he's not going?' What sort of loving wife could I be to force this dear man to go somewhere he didn't want to go? I bit my lip as he settled into the seat. Once again his face pressed against the window, once more his eyes glistened with tears. He waved, I waved, and the taxi drove away.

I cried for half an hour then, with difficulty, gathered my thoughts, got ready and set off in the car. I had to admit it did me good; just for a short while I could think of something else. I had coffee in a café, read the paper and tried to relax. I pottered around the shops picking up some essentials and treated myself to a new skirt.

I headed for home just after noon, part of my mind wondering how Eddie was managing as I got closer and closer to home. I just about convinced myself that he'd be better with his second session. Holding onto those thoughts, I walked into the house.

There were two messages waiting on the answering machine, both from the day-care centre. The first was: 'Mrs Huck, could you ring us as soon as you get this message?' The second, which had arrived just a few minutes before I got home: 'Mrs Huck, could you come and pick Eddie up as soon as possible, please?'

I was shaking as I dashed back out of the house, fell into the car seat and raced off.

CHAPTER 5

'I'M A TRAINED NURSE, I CAN COPE'

Anyone who embarks on a similar journey will discover that there are no maps to follow. There will be advice, encouragement and varying degrees of help from professionals, family and friends. As I've said, no two journeys are the same: some are prolonged, slowly changing over many years; others rush along like a river in flood. We struggle through as best we can.

Our main strength is love. Love keeps us going when courage fails; love is there in the middle of the night when the long hours of darkness stretch ahead. Love holds us together when hope has gone, and it is love that carries us through to the end.

I'm sure I drove too fast to the centre. Whatever had happened? Had Eddie fallen and hurt himself? No, they would have said so in the message. I should have phoned before I left but I didn't want to waste any time. Get there – get there fast.

As I turned down the final lane, I was still shaking. I felt responsible for whatever had happened. Eddie hadn't wanted to go and I should have listened. But, oh no, I wanted a break. I wanted to go swanning off for a bit of unimportant shopping. It was my fault. I shouldn't have agreed to the day care. In those last few hundred yards to the centre, I called myself every word of condemnation imaginable.

When I arrived, Eddie was standing outside on the pavement, waving his stick, threatening to bash the two carers who were trying to hold onto him! One was the foreign gentleman who had come to the house for the original assessment; the other was a young girl who worked there. They kept having to dodge back as the stick whirled past their heads. 'Let me go! Get out of it! Shove off!' were the words that I heard as I stopped the car.

'He's become rather upset,' said the man, an understatement in the circumstances. He ducked as the stick narrowly missed him. 'He was okay up to an hour ago but he's been getting more agitated. That's why we phoned you.'

'Get off! You buggers! Damn you!' The stick whirled again and Eddie nearly overbalanced as he tried to aim a kick at the girl. 'I'm going to report you. I know what you're up to! Go on, get off!'

I leapt out of the car and caught his arm. Keep calm, I told myself. Don't get upset. 'Come on, Eddie, time to go home.'

'These buggers are trying to kill me,' he insisted, backing away from them but keeping the stick raised like a weapon.

'Come on, get in the car. Let's have you home,' I urged. He was muttering and cursing as I managed to get him into the passenger seat.

'Bye, Eddie,' they said, backing away, obviously relieved. I didn't waste any time in conversation, I just restarted the engine and drove.

'Take me to the police station, Jackie. Right now, to the police station, I've got to tell them. This lot are coming back tonight. They're going to kill me!' His face was red with anger, his fists balled. 'The buggers, they're nothing but bloody buggers,' he kept repeating.

'The police station's closed for the day. We'll have to phone when we get home,' I lied, heading out into the country.

'Are you in with them?' he questioned, now turning his face to me.

'No, love, I'm on your side. We'll tell the police all about them as soon as we get home.'

I took my time and let him ramble. He called the day-centre staff every expletive he knew but it wasn't just anger; he was obviously terrified.

'They'll be round tonight,' he said. 'Soon as we get in, we'll have to make sure all the windows are closed and the doors locked. Perhaps we should go away for the night, then we won't be there when they come.'

'I don't think they'll come, they'll be too busy.'

'Oh no, they're coming. We must get the police to protect us.'

We were half way home and he was still ranting. I tried changing the subject. 'Goodness the sky's going dark, I think it's going to rain. Did you speak to your Bobby today?'

But Eddie was having none of it. 'Our Bobby's back in Melton. He's well out of it, he can't help. No, we'll have to get the police. The bloody buggers, they'll be round soon as it gets dark. If it rains they'll like it because we won't see them. We'll have to keep look-out. Are they following?' He spun round in the passenger seat, straining to see if there was a car behind. Thankfully the road was clear.

By the time we arrived home, I didn't know what to say or do. He was still swearing and shaking his fists, demanding I phone the police. I pretended to make a phone call, wondering what I should say. I held an imaginary conversation with a policeman as Eddie hovered beside me. 'No, Sergeant, they're not here yet, but my husband is sure they'll be coming later.' I nodded for effect as Eddie watched. 'Yes, we'll keep the doors locked. Thank you. We'll see you soon.'

Eddie was pacing, waving his stick around again; it was obviously more weapon than support for the time being. 'Are the police coming?' he asked.

'Yes, but it could be a while. They've got a lot of calls to make.'

We spent the next hour up and down stairs, checking rooms, opening doors, looking in cupboards. We drew curtains then opened them again. We checked the doors were locked over and over again. I could see he was starting to get tired. 'Shall we have a drink?' I asked as he sat down in the living room, still clutching his stick.

He nodded, I filled the kettle and put on the television. 'We can watch the news while we wait. You like to know what's happening in the world, but it's usually all bad.' I babbled on, jumping from subject to subject, talking about the weather, the cats and the village.

He sipped his tea and, for the first time in a while, grew quiet. I offered him a ginger biscuit, his favourite; he dunked it silently, savouring the taste. His stick slipped unnoticed onto the carpet. One of the cats climbed onto his knee and Eddie's fingers ruffled through the soft fur.

The tea drunk, he focused his attention on the news and the programme that followed. I slipped off his shoes, lit the Rayburn and made the evening meal. Slowly calm descended and Eddie started to talk about the cows and some news item he'd just watched. It was as if a blanket of peace was thrown over his shoulders and he relaxed. As violently as it had come, the agitation went; the fear was forgotten and with it the police.

It had taken nearly four hours for him to calm down.

Analysing the situation later, the whole episode struck me as rather bizarre. Eddie had gone to a day-care centre run by the Alzheimer's Society, in other words run by the experts. These were the people who dealt with different dementia problems on a daily basis. These were the professionals who knew how to handle difficult situations but, when a problem had arisen, I had been left to sort it out. No one had telephoned to make sure everything was alright. Eddie had been dumped back into my lap and, for better or for worse, I'd been expected to cope. Thankfully I had, and the situation had gradually cooled down, but when Eddie had climbed back in the car he had been in a violent, agitated state.

I suppose it was expected that he would quieten down in the company of someone he knew and trusted – but no one knew for sure and certainly no one checked that was the case. What if Eddie had grown more violent? We could have had a car crash or he could have walloped me with his stick. One thing was certain: at least for the time being, that was the end of day care!

Eddie was seventy-nine on the 3rd October. After our customary uneasy night, he was awake around 8.30. I washed and dressed him, secured his pad and string pants, which he now needed during the day as well, and got him downstairs for breakfast. The social worker was due the next day and, since the 'day-care crisis', life had been relatively quiet. I'd decided to leave things lie until she came.

I'd invested in a special chair a few weeks before. I'd had increasing problems on days when Eddie's mobility was poor. Once he sank himself down in his armchair, he had great difficulty getting out of it. I'd had back problems on and off for years and had to be so careful about lifting and bending. I was already forced to do a certain amount of hauling Eddie around, but I'd decided a special electrically-operated chair would make life a bit easier.

Eddie had found it great fun. It had a special hand-control box, which tucked neatly into the chair pocket, and arrows indicating which way you wanted the chair to go. The 'up' button gently raised the seat to bring Eddie into a standing position; the 'down' button made the chair go as flat as desired, almost like a bed. Plus, the foot area could be raised independently so he could put his feet up. 'It's like being at the fairground,' he'd say, as the chair 'upped' and 'downed'. We were always getting the buttons confused to great hilarity, going up when we wanted to be down,.

I got him into his chair, gave him his birthday card, a box of his favourite chocolates and a big kiss.

'Is it my birthday?' he asked in surprise, struggling to open my card with the others he'd received. 'Fancy me forgetting. How old am I this year?'

'How old do you think you are?' I asked.

'Oh, I must have turned sixty. Sixty-one, sixty-two?' he guessed.

'That's right, love,' I assured him, passing him the newspaper and his glasses.

***

I'd been a member of the Scribblers writing group for a few years and really enjoyed the meetings. It was just a small group held in various members' homes in a hamlet a twenty-minute drive away, and they had said it was fine to take Eddie with me. That afternoon he was okay; his mobility was good for a change and he sat listening contentedly. Everyone wished him happy birthday and he tucked into the proffered tea and biscuits. Once back home, he was tired and settled in his chair. I raised the footrest and he had a doze.

That evening was the annual harvest supper at the market hall. I'd left it open-ended whether we went or not, depending on what sort of a day Eddie was having. Fortunately, after his sleep he was fine.

'Where are we going?' he asked, as I got him ready.

'Harvest supper. There'll be a good feed on and some entertainment.'

'Great. Will our Bobby be there?'

'Let's hope so, love.'

It was a fine evening for October; I always used to joke with Eddie that he had better weather for his birthday than I had for mine in May. We parked outside the hall so he only had a short walk inside. He was soon seated at a table with lots of well-known faces from the village around him. As always, the food was lovely, all home-made and as much as anyone could eat.

We sat with Marion and Arty and other people Eddie knew. He chatted constantly, quite often going off on some strange tack but everyone played along. After the meal and before the entertainment, it was announced that it was Eddie's birthday. Everyone in the packed room sang 'Happy Birthday' with gusto. Eddie's eyes welled with tears. As they finished, he stood up. In a voice choking with emotion, he thanked them all. It was to be the last time Eddie went to Orton market hall and, for many in that room, the last time they saw him.

Rachel, the social worker, arrived the next day and listened quietly as I explained what had happened at day care. 'How much sleep are you getting?' she asked.

I told her it was about the same, three to five hours broken into chunks. I started welling up again as I talked; these damn tears, they were becoming uncontrollable.

'You really must start to think about Eddie going in for

respite care,' she urged. 'If your health breaks down, he'll have to go because you'll have no choice.'

Fighting tears I tried to think, but the vivid memory of Eddie waving his stick around outside the day-care centre filled my mind. If he could work himself up like that in just a few hours, whatever would he be like left for a week in an unfamiliar place with strangers? I would never be able to explain to him; he'd think he'd been abandoned and betrayed. No, no, I couldn't do it.

I turned away so Eddie wouldn't see me cry. 'I can manage.'

Was it that evening or the next? So much has become blurred by time. Eddie had eaten his tea and was watching the television when, as on so many occasions, he made his 'Well, time we were away home' comment. His legs had been good that day so into the car we went for a trip over the moors to 'come home'. Back in the house for around 8pm, off with the coat and boots, and back into the chair. An hour later, we were off again, this time on a ten-mile round trip in the opposite direction. Each time after he'd 'come home', he settled for a while. After the second trip, I hoped he would be content and go to bed later.

It was edging towards eleven when Eddie stood up. 'Are you ready for bed, love?' I asked.

'No. We haven't put Johnny into the stable. It's going cold and he hasn't a blanket.'

'Johnny?'

'The old horse, of course. Come on, we'll go and find him.'

As we wrapped up, I grabbed a torch. Thankfully it was a pleasant evening, chilly, with only a slight wind and not raining. Our farmhouse lies on the edge of the village, and we have an outside light which illuminates the side of the house.

Down the yard towards the old cowshed there is some light from the last of the village street lights, plus the buildings have lights inside, but head up the yard and it is black. Off Eddie went, up the yard towards the fields, me keeping pace shining the torch.

Looking back, it was a surreal experience walking by torch and a little starlight into this all-enveloping night. The old calving sheds merged into the blackness, somewhere an owl was hooting and, as we left the shelter of the buildings, the rustle of wind in tree and grass gathered around us. I kept hold of Eddie's arm, terrified he might fall because there was no way I could pick him up. As we turned right towards the field at the side of our top hay meadow, the ground underfoot became muddy and uneven.

We reached the gate, which is difficult to open in daylight, the chain grown rusty and stiff. Eddie strained at the fastening, having to lift the metal gate for the hook to clear. He was still amazingly strong, his big farmer's hands still capable of heavy work. 'He was somewhere in this field last I saw him,' he said, as the gate swung open.

Now we plodded on into the empty field, like an expedition into the abyss. The clouds must have been gathering as the last starlight vanished. People who live in towns, cannot imagine the complete cloak of night when there is no light anywhere, plus the stillness broken only by the voice of wind. I shone the torch around, lighting nothing but grass and distant stone walls.

'Johnny! Johnny!' shouted Eddie. 'I should have brought a bucket with some feed,' he added, as we ploughed over humps and bumps in the land, somehow managing to keep our footing. 'Johnny! Johnny!' he kept on calling as we plodded back and forward on this pointless hunt.

'I think he's up there,' said Eddie. I'd shone the torch over to a far wall and something had moved – a bird? 'Johnny! Come on old chap! Johnny!'

I hung on to Eddie's arm as he forged his way across the field, now something like a hundred yards from the gate. We reached the wall and found nothing but stone and more grass. 'I was sure I saw him. Johnny! Johnny!'

'I don't think he's here, love. Let's go back, it's getting cold,' I urged. I shone the torch on my watch: 11.30.

'I hope he'll be alight,' said Eddie, reluctantly turning back the way we'd come. Guided by the torch, we found our way back to the gate, thankfully without mishap. 'My legs are getting a bit tired,' he conceded as he lurched. I managed to steady him and slowly we struggled back to the house. As we neared the door, Eddie said, 'What we doing out here in the cold, Jackie?'

I felt like saying looking for an old plough horse which has been dead for over sixty years, but I was just so relieved to have Eddie back safe in the house that all I said was, 'Goodness knows. Let's get you to bed.'

We went to see Eddie's sister, Ruby, the next day. She was deeply worried about his deteriorating state of mind as Eddie persisted in asking her where their Bobby was. Ruby told him he was in the graveyard but the realisation that his brother was dead only brought tears; Eddie was far better lost in his fantasies.

It was a few days later when Eddie vanished! We were having a good spell of autumn weather and I'd been pottering around the garden while Eddie was busy tinkering in his workshop. At this stage, his mobility was still variable: one day he could barely get out of a chair, or walk any distance even with his stick; another day he would be up and down the yard without difficulty. I can't remember who it was, but a friend popped round and we spent about twenty minutes chatting in the garden. It did cross my mind if Eddie was okay but, since he was having a good day and I'd left him busy, I didn't worry.

As soon as I was alone, I went into his workshop to see if he was ready for a cup of tea. It was deserted.

I didn't panic at first; there were lots of places he could be so I started hunting. First the house: I went through every room, up and down stairs, round the back and front gardens and through the small gate that leads from the rear garden into the nearby field. No sign. On to all the outbuildings; that's the thing with farms – lots of bits of buildings. I checked every nook of the old cowshed, into the neglected milking parlour where the busy machinery used to be, next door into a storage area. Then up the yard into the tractor shed, the tool shed, across to the unused calving pens: nothing.

I tried the tiny lane between the fields, looking over walls, negotiating fallen tree trunks, prowling down an overgrown path round the back of neighbouring houses: nothing. I shouted his name but no answer came; because of his deafness he wouldn't have been able to hear me. It was after three. In an hour it would be getting dark, the cold was creeping on and rain was threatening. Yes, I was starting to panic. Where could he be? I felt I was to blame; I should have been watching him.

As on many other occasions when emergency struck, I phoned Marion. She answered: Arty would come. He was there a few minutes later.

'I'll check the bottom fields first,' he said. 'If I can't find him, I'll go up the top fields.' Off he went, while I continued round the back of the old mill, down the lane, in and out of already-checked buildings. Could he have doubled back? Might he have fallen behind something? With his lack of peripheral vision, he could so easily fall. Should I phone the police? I fought for calm, my heart hammering.

It was twilight. Arty was still hunting and I was on the brink of calling the police. What would they do? Call in the mountain rescue? What if they didn't find him by dark? It was forecasting frost tonight; he'd get hypothermia. To say I was in turmoil was an understatement. Then, as I hurried up the yard, he appeared through the gate.

I wanted to hug and thump him all at the same time. He'd only got a thin jacket over his jumper. Everything he wore was soaking and he'd only been wearing light shoes, so his feet and legs were covered in wet mud. He met me with a wide grin. 'Well, I don't know where I've been but I'm back.'

Just then Arty turned up, as relieved as me to see the wanderer safe home. 'I'll get him dried out and warmed up,' I said, thanking Arty for helping.

'Any time. Don't hesitate.'

Eddie was obviously exhausted and it was an effort to get him up to the bathroom. I stripped off his wet clothes, washed and rubbed to get him clean, and redressed him in warm clothes. It would have been better to have got him into the bath but he was having increasing trouble getting in and out.

Back downstairs, clutching a hot drink, I tried to find out where he'd been. 'I went up to check on those cows in the top fields,' he said, 'but I must have missed them.' He scratched his head puzzled; he'd walked this land all his life. 'I don't know what happened. I got in the long grass then fell in a big puddle. But I came back, that's what matters.'

We laughed it off and I was just so relieved he was alright. I'd had visions of a night hunt by torchlight, perhaps asking the local villagers and farmers to help. I'd imagined a helicopter, fire brigade and ambulance, the press descending; in fact, in the hour or more he was missing I imagined every awful scenario possible, including Eddie being found injured or dead and being carted down the yard on a stretcher. My abiding thought that evening was thank God he's okay.

I received a phone call on Thursday 6th October from the Alzheimer's Society chap. How was Eddie? I assured him he was about the same and hadn't got worked up since his last day-care session.

'He was fine in the morning,' the man said. 'It was after lunch he started to get agitated. Rachel phoned me to see if it was worth having another try. What do you think?' After the last debacle, I had my doubts. 'You could go and get some shopping done, the break will do you good. But I think we'd better have Eddie just until after lunch. Could you pick him up at 1pm?'

I nearly said no, then the 'Eddie's gone missing' affair jumped out at me. For how long now would I be able to leave him alone? An hour? Half an hour? Ten or five minutes? I could take him with me down to the local shop but he'd never be able to walk round town, and there's only so much you can buy locally. Two mornings a week, if it worked out, was better than nothing. I hesitated, weighing the pros and cons.

'Give it a go on Monday,' he prompted. 'If it doesn't work, well, at least we've tried.' Reluctantly I agreed, after leaving him my mobile phone number and instructions to phone me immediately if there was trouble.

The weekend passed in our usual merry-go-round manner. By day I went hour by hour, ticking off the hours of daylight, dreading darkness. The weather deteriorated and the temperature dropped. Eddie's legs tired easily and even walking down the yard became an effort. During the day he used the outside toilet so he didn't have to go upstairs; it was handy to the house but meant going outside in the rain. I had to accompany him on each visit, watching he didn't fall as there were two small steps to negotiate. Soon we'd need a downstairs commode and possibly a wheelchair.

At bedtime I worked out a system to get him upstairs using two chairs. Our staircase rises six steps then has a flat area before turning left for the final steps to the landing. I put one chair on the first flat area and I had my old office chair up on the top. He could manage to pull himself up to the first chair using the handrails, with me supporting him from behind. Then, after a rest on the chair, we used the same method to reach the landing. Once on the swivel chair, which was on castors, I could push him most of the way down the landing and get him to the bathroom and bedroom. Quite a performance, but for the time being it worked.

'It's like pushing an old cow around,' Eddie would say amid laughter, as we made our slow ascent up Jacob's Ladder.

He still was determined to 'go home' most evenings, so we'd dress up in wet-weather gear and splash through the rain to the car. Round the village we'd drive, sometimes up the Scar, the window-wipers on fast speed trying to cope with the deluge.

Sunday evening, Eddie was convinced we were expecting a delivery of sheep. 'Come on, our Ruby, we're meeting the wagon down at the service station,' he said, heading for the door in his slippers.

By this time I was used to being addressed by a variety of names. 'We're getting some sheep?' I asked.

'You know damn well we are, a full wagon load. We're wintering them. I spent all yesterday making sure the walls and gates are secure and we had that feed delivered. Come on, they'll be waiting.'

I persuaded him to put on his Wellingtons and don a

jacket then, with me steadying one side and his stick on the other, we got to the car. It was bucketing it down as we headed off.

'Get a move on,' he said as I drove slowly, hoping he'd forget where we were going. 'They're bringing them to the service-station parking area and then we'll guide them up to the farm.' Argument would have proved fruitless, so off we went.

As we pulled into the car park, Eddie looked around. 'I don't think they're here yet. Just drive down the other end to make sure.'

I did as I was asked then we parked up to wait. I kept the engine running with the heater on and left the window wipers busy trying to cope with the increasing rain, which was turning to sleet. The wind buffeted the car as the minutes ticked away.

'They're late. Perhaps we should head down the motorway and look for them,' said Eddie.

I really didn't fancy a magical-mystery tour in that weather. I wracked my brain for a solution. 'Let's phone them,' I said. 'See where they are.' He agreed it was a good idea. I pulled out my mobile and proceeded to make an imaginary phone call. If I remember, it went something along these lines: 'Oh, is that the sheep delivery man? Good. Where are you? We're waiting. Oh dear! But you're okay? Thank goodness for that. Yes. Yes.' (Nodding) 'I'll tell him. Fine, we'll see you in the morning.'

'What's happened?' asked Eddie, concerned.

'They've been held up. There's been an accident on the motorway with this weather, and there's a big tailback. He's going to stay down below Preston for the night and set off again in the morning.'

'But the sheep can't stay in the wagon all night, they'll

need feeding,' said Eddie, starting to get upset.

I didn't realise I was such a good liar. 'Oh, don't worry, he's offloading them at a farm for the night. It's all taken care of.' Eddie sighed with relief and dried his eyes. 'Can we go home now?' I asked. He agreed and we turned around for home.

Once back in the house, he settled to the television and his evening meal and never mentioned the sheep again.

I got Eddie up early on Monday; thankfully he was having one of his bright, good-leg mornings. Over breakfast I broached the subject of the day care, praying he'd forgotten about his last visit. He had.

The taxi was due just after 9am. 'Where are we going?' asked Eddie, as I put on his outdoor shoes and helped him into his jacket.

'You're just going over to the centre for a few hours. You can take your paper and read it and I've got a farming magazine for you,' I said. 'I'll be along to pick you up after lunch.'

I'd been down this particular troubled path before with alarming results, but on this occasion he took it all in his stride, chatting to the driver as he helped him into the taxi. He waved as it drove down the yard but he seemed content and there were no tears. This made me feel better so, armed with my shopping list and mobile phone, I headed into town.

It turned out to be an uneventful day. The phone never rang and, although it was a bit of a rush, I arrived promptly at 1pm to pick up Eddie. 'He's been fine,' the Alzheimer's care leader, assured me as Eddie thanked them for lunch and was helped into the car. I heaved a sigh of relief; at least this time all had been well, but would it last?

Nurse Maggie came at 1pm on Wednesday 12th October. After a quiet day before, we'd had an awful night. Eddie had been almost off his legs and I'd had terrible trouble getting him upstairs; we'd been up about twelve times during the night. If his legs were bad during the day, they were worse in the cold, dark hours of early morning. Even with incontinence pad and pants, it was not unusual to change the bed three times during the night. The problem of getting an eleven-stone man out of a wet bed into my office chair on castors and into the bathroom to the loo umpteen times in the middle of the night cannot be overstated.

Nurse Maggie took one look at me and said, 'You must think about respite care. If you don't have a break, you're going to be ill.' Naturally I cried as she made some phone calls. 'I've made arrangements for Eddie to go into Sunnygarth on Friday for a week. They have a special unit there and he'll be fine.' I carried on crying.

Eddie was sitting in his chair watching the news while all this was going on. Since I was behind him, and because of his deafness, he was unaware of both the conversation and tears. 'He's managing day care again,' I said between sobs. 'If we have a commode by the bed, that will help. I'm a trained nurse, I can cope.'

Maggie put her arm around me. 'For how long? If you have a week's break and get some sleep, you'll feel more able. Really,' she urged.

I took some convincing. However could I tell Eddie? He wouldn't understand and he'd be afraid. Round and round I went as the tears continued.

Maggie went and sat with him. 'You'd not mind a little holiday, would you, Eddie?' she asked.

He looked puzzled. 'Are we going somewhere?' he asked.

'Yes, just you for a few days. Your Jackie's not well, she needs a rest.'

'Can't she come?' he asked. Oh God! This was awful!!

That's how it was left. 'Don't worry,' said Maggie, as she drove away. 'You'll see, it will work out.'

I got even less sleep that night; if I wasn't toileting, I was worrying.

The second day-care session the following day went off without trouble and I explained to the staff that Eddie wouldn't be there the next week. As he settled himself in the car for the drive home he said, 'I'm not going there again. I don't know who the hell they all are but they're all batty.' I didn't bother telling him that he didn't have to go for at least a week because he would be away in a care home.

I developed a headache worrying about the following day. I went upstairs to pack him a case, more tears dripping onto his pyjamas. It had been decided I would take him into Sunnygarth the next morning by car – but how was I going to explain to him where he was going and why he had to stay? The more I worried, the more I became convinced I just couldn't do it. But did I have a choice? Perhaps Maggie was right: how much longer could I cope with little bits of broken-up sleep?

The phone was ringing as I came downstairs from packing. It was the manager of Sunnygarth care home. I don't remember her name and we'd never met. She asked me if I was Mrs Huck and was it true that my husband was coming in the next day for emergency respite care. I told her yes, that Nurse Maggie had arranged it.

The gist of the conversation which followed was that she'd been off duty the day it had been arranged, and there was no way she was going to have Eddie at Sunnygarth! He hadn't been assessed by them and they were not equipped to cope with a patient like him. I suppose it was her manner but she seemed quite put-out by the whole affair. She made me feel like I'd caused her a lot of inconvenience and trouble; she was polite but firm – Eddie was not to come!

So, that was that. Having gone through the trauma of coming round to allowing him to go from my care for a week, with all the implications of that, it wasn't going to happen. I hadn't wanted it anyway, and in many ways I was relieved. It obviously wasn't to be. I'd managed so far and I would continue – but there had to be some changes to enable me to look after Eddie.

I spent that evening and a good part of the night 'mulling'. By morning I had a new plan, one which I was convinced would work. There was no way my gentle, loving husband was going into a home. I was a trained nurse – I could cope!!

CHAPTER 6

CRISIS POINT

I awoke the next day with a new determination. I would move the bedroom downstairs so the staircase would no longer be a problem. Also I would need a commode, a wheelchair and washing facilities.

Living in an old farmhouse, we were lucky in having a number of downstairs rooms. The middle room had been my mother's bedroom for the last few years of her life so I would convert it into a bedroom again. There was another room beyond it where the furniture could be stored; all I needed now was some manpower. This was supplied by Nick, our neighbour, and Craig, a farming friend and Arty's son. Could they come and help? No problem; they came later that day.

All unnecessary items, including a large table, chairs and a display cabinet, were moved out. Downstairs came two single beds, bedside table, lamps and an old washstand we had in the bathroom. This sounds like an easy manoeuvre but my two knights in shining armour needed to be both patient and strong. It's not easy to hump furniture around in old property with strange narrow corridors, low ceilings and a twisting staircase but, after quite a lot of manoeuvring, they managed.

I'd telephoned Maggie about a commode and she said she'd leave a prescription at the chemist in town if someone could go and pick it up. She'd also been really angry about the reaction of the manager at Sunnygarth, but we let that lie for the present.

Oh, the comfort and support of good friends! Marion rushed off in her van to pick up the commode, and I phoned Jan, another friend, who had a wheelchair she could lend us. The final preparations were a washing-up bowl to go on the washstand, Eddie's shaving mirror and equipment put ready with soap and towels, and a bucket. I felt a sense of satisfaction when everything was in place. This would work – this had to work!

How do I write about the next few weeks? I've been working up to this chapter since I started writing about the journey and, as I faced the telling, I almost gave up. Looking back, I was filled with new hope when we moved downstairs; for the first time in weeks I felt in control of the situation. We were now on one level and, even if Eddie's legs got worse, it was surely a simple matter of moving him around via the wheelchair.

At first all seemed well. Eddie accepted the move without question, in fact he thought it rather funny. Since the day care had been cancelled for the following week, I left it that way; it was one problem less to deal with. As chance would have it, Eddie was having a 'good leg' day so we took advantage of this to go 'hut' hunting.

During the late summer we'd had the old greenhouse taken down; it was falling to pieces anyway and I suggested buying a small summerhouse to replace it. We'd had a number of summers where there had been a cold wind blowing even on a sunny day and it was impossible to sit out of doors. An outdoor hut would mean we could sit in the warmth but still enjoy the garden.

I'd hunted through the local papers and on the internet to

see what was available in the area and we set off to see what we could find. I remember that day as one of happy adventure, laughing and chatting as we went to three different places to see what they had on offer and compare prices. Some were astronomical. 'We're not after Buckingham Palace,' Eddie chuckled.

We settled on a medium-sized wooden structure with windows in the double doors and two other front windows, one each side. It was large enough to fit in a couple of chairs and a table, but small enough to fit the space vacated by the greenhouse. We ordered and paid for it, and made arrangements for it to be delivered and built on-site the following week.

I suppose I was being optimistic expecting it to last. Thinking that the problems were solved, making myself believe that Eddie's slight improvement would continue. When you've taught yourself to live hour by hour, that's how you move on. A bad morning or night is discounted as a glitch; it's pushed behind you, forgotten, and you carry on ticking off the good hours, never looking too far ahead.

Nurse Maggie arrived on Thursday October 20th and approved of the new bedroom. She asked how everything was working. We'd been downstairs for almost a week and I'd been settling to a new routine. Eddie was still needing the toilet many times during the night and I could now transfer him to the bedside commode. If he'd wet the bed, I sat him out while I changed him and the bed. In the morning I filled the kettle with hot water, poured some into the plastic bowl while he sat in front of the washstand. I helped him to wash and shave, then I emptied the water into a bucket for disposal. Lastly, depending on how bad his legs were that morning, I dressed him, then he either walked with support or I wheeled him through to the living room. Yes, it was working fine – but was it?

We'd solved the staircase problem but all the other problems still remained. In some ways, they were exaggerated. As his bed was now handy in the next-door room, Eddie was constantly going to bed. He'd have breakfast, read his paper, watch a bit of television and then decide it was bedtime. This wasn't helped by the dark, drizzly days. Convinced it was evening, he was determined to go to bed. So I'd take him back into the bedroom, he'd undress and go to bed. I'd either stay in the room reading or I'd keep looking back in. An hour or two later, it was 'getting-up time'. I'd dress him again, bring him back into the front room, only for us to start the whole performance again an hour or two later. This went on all day, into the evening and sometimes into the early hours of the morning. Meals were pushed in between with difficulty. I'd be preparing something and he'd be either struggling out of his chair (off to bed) or climbing out of bed (getting up)! If I set a meal on the table, many times he refused it. 'But I've only just eaten,' he'd say.

In Eddie's mind we were frequently having problems with the German prisoners at Shap Wells. He'd pull himself out of his chair announcing, 'I can't be sitting here, we're on guard tonight.' I'd try to reassure him they were secure. 'Are they all asleep?' he'd ask; he was only content to settle after I'd looked in the hall to check everyone was locked up.

I was never sure why he kept returning to this subject. All I could surmise was that, because he was a boy during the Second World War, it must have been exciting to think that Germans were being imprisoned only a few miles away. Also, they could be seen marching through the village under escort. It must have made a deep impression and, as Eddie's mind reverted back in time, these embedded memories resurfaced in a distorted manner.

Sadly, the psychotic events were increasing. If I managed to sit him down for breakfast, I'd see him emptying his tablets into his handkerchief and hiding them in his pocket. When I asked why, he'd sneer at me. 'I know you're poisoning me,' he'd say. Denial was useless; all I could do was wait and hope he'd take them later in the day when he'd forgotten about the fantasy.

On days when his legs were steadier, his mobility was so changeable during this period that he quite often tried to escape! Convinced I was preparing to knife or shoot him, he'd wait until my back was turned then try to be off. Thankfully the alarms alerted me if he went through either of the outside doors. Usually I kept these locked and the keys hidden but if someone had been to the door, or I'd gone out for coal, it was so easy to forget to relock or reset the alarm.

I had to be constantly on guard. Because of the alarm system, I'd discover his disappearance quickly and I'd be off, no matter what the weather, chasing after him. He never got far, just down or up the yard. Then I'd follow him round, flapping about in soaking slippers.

One occasion it was pigs he was after. He'd kept pigs for a number of years before we'd met. There had been a programme on the television about keeping pigs in the Lake District so, of course, Eddie had pigs again. Such a hunt we had that day looking for these invisible pigs, Eddie clutching a small bail of straw he'd found, determined to bed them down against the cold.

Sometimes he would manage to 'escape' somewhere in the house. I would leave the living room for just a few minutes and return to find him gone. I'd check that the doors were locked before hunting around the house. He was adept at finding hiding places, especially upstairs. I suppose in his own mind it was the kind of hide-and-seek he played when he was a small boy. I could find him tucked behind a bed, in the airing cupboard or concealed in some obscure corner. When found, sometimes he'd come out laughing, the reason he'd hidden forgotten; at other times he would shrink with fear or become angry.

I suppose matters were gradually building up to a crisis. It had been coming for months as I resisted the truth. I'd been warned by Nurse Maggie and the social worker but, especially after the move downstairs, I was sure I could carry on.

Eddie returned to the day-care centre on Monday 24th. I'd assured him it was only for a few hours, and I'd be along at 1pm after lunch. He went without question but his legs were getting weaker again and he needed a wheelchair from house to taxi.

After he'd gone I bumbled around the house, going over and over all the problems, before going to see Judy, who lived in the village. She had spoken to me a number of times since Eddie had been diagnosed as she was a retired nurse who had worked for many years with dementia patients. Her own mother and father had both suffered from dementia, so she knew the problems.

She'd come across to the house one evening to try and help when Eddie was having a bad psychotic attack but Eddie didn't know her. I'd discovered that he'd only calm down for people he knew well, but on this occasion no one was available. Judy had said to phone any time and I was in a desperate state that night. Eddie was getting angry and on the point of violence, determined I would kill him. Sadly Judy didn't manage to help in the way she wished as Eddie became even more agitated, turning his fear and suspicions on her, saying she'd come to murder him. Then he turned to me for protection, so in a strange way it had sorted itself out.

I had to talk to someone so, over a cup of tea, I poured out both my heart and a lot more tears. She listened sympathetically. 'You're going to have to let him go into respite care,' she said.

'Sunnygarth won't have him and I don't think I could go through all that anguish again.'

'What about Silverdown where I used to work? We could go and have a look round.'

My instant words and thoughts were: 'No! No! He must stay at home; I must carry on coping.'

'Just let me take you to see the place and meet the staff. They also do day care.' Still I resisted but said I'd think about it. 'What about going over on Thursday, when Eddie's at the centre?' she urged. 'If you want to go, phone me on Thursday morning.' And that was how it was left.

I think back with difficulty; memory can be kind and tries to block out mental pain. I realise at that time my mind was in disarray, weighing possibilities, pushing aside unwanted facts, but the truth kept returning like an ominous cloud.

I couldn't guarantee at any point of any day or night what Eddie's mood or mobility would be. The next two nights were terrible: he was in and out of bed every hour, tearing off his pad, resulting in soaking sheets. He found it difficult to stand, so I had to support him in and out of bed, struggling to get him onto a chair or commode.

By Thursday I ached all over and was exhausted. With difficulty I got him up and dressed for day care and, with the help of the driver, managed to help him into the taxi. Again he went without trouble but I had to be there to pick him up by one.

I was shaking when I phoned Judy. 'Okay, I'll take a look at Silverdown.'

As she drove, we made inconsequential conversation. I

became more worked up as we neared the home, a twenty-five minute drive. I'd never been down that lane before, having passed the turning without thought on many occasions. The car headed through a small village with a number of trim houses on one side and a wall and trees on the other, which flanked a different care home. 'They used to be under the same ownership but it was sold some time ago. It's a general nursing home,' said Judy. 'Silverdown's an EMI unit.'

As I came to write about this journey, I realised I'd forgotten what EMI stands for. I know Judy told me but I was in no condition to remember and afterwards it didn't seem to matter. I looked it up on the Internet and it means Elderly Mental Impaired. It's a term which isn't being used as much now, but it signified a secure care home which deals with patients suffering from all forms of dementia. Many care homes have a separate unit but Silverdown was specifically designed for dementia sufferers. Secure literally means 'locked', for the safety of the patients.

My heart was pounding as we turned into the drive and crunched over the chippings into the car park.

It was a modern building, constructed some years before. A neat flower bed lay in the courtyard. Judy led the way as we headed up to the main door and into the small exterior vestibule. There was a book on a table for visitors to sign in, a hand-sanitizer and button on the wall marked 'Press for attention'. Through the inner glass door I could see a large seating area with patients and carers.

Seeing us, one of the girls came over, entered the code and opened the door. 'Hello, Judy, how's things?' she said with a smile as Judy introduced me.

We stepped in and the door relocked itself behind us. An elderly woman with an agonised look on her face stood nearby clutching her wrongly buttoned cardigan. 'Bloody hell! Bloody hell!' she muttered as she walked away.

The warmth was welcoming after the outside cold but the heating was set higher than a normal house and I could already feel the sweat prickling. An aroma drifted on the warm air, one I remembered from my days of nursing, that institutional smell visitors always speak about that becomes unnoticeable when you work in it daily.

There must have been about fifteen patients scattered around the sitting room, some in chairs, others tottering around with varying degrees of steadiness. There were five staff visible, some giving out mid-morning refreshments from a well-laden trolley, others busy helping and encouraging patients to drink and eat the proffered biscuits. One patient was throwing bits of biscuit back at the nurse, who kept trying to persuade him to eat. Another lady returned her full cup to the trolley, upending the contents; the warm liquid sopped around as a carer quickly mopped it up.

Soft music was playing in the background; though the easy chairs were a mismatched bunch they looked comfy, and there was a scattering of cushions and soft toys. All these and many more impressions floated around me as we made our way to the office, where Judy introduced me to Carol, the manager.

'I'll leave you to talk,' said Judy. 'I'll go and catch up with the staff.'

Tea and biscuits were brought as I settled into a chair. The office was small, with a glass window overlooking the sitting room. Files and books were stacked around. I sipped tea as the manager asked me about Eddie.

At first I was quite controlled, outlining the development of Eddie's dementia over the last year, telling her about the night-time problems, the increasing confusion and the psychotic attacks. She probed gently, easing out of me the trauma of dealing with everything that was happening twenty-four hours a day. As I talked the tears started – oh, those wretched tears – then I was sobbing.

It was a while before I managed to gain my composure. I apologised and mopped my face.

'Don't worry and don't apologise,' Carol said. 'Would you like to look round?'

I agreed, and we made our way out of the office.

'This is the dining room.' Carol indicated a pleasant room between the sitting room and kitchen. I followed as we crossed the room where I'd come in, heading for the staircase. 'Every resident has their own room. We're in the process of redecorating and refurbishing. I'll show you a room that's recently been completed.'

We reached the top of the staircase. There was another security panel where she entered a code to open the door. A short walk along the landing, past another small sitting room. 'The patients on the upper level are usually less mobile than those downstairs and they need total nursing care as well as special dementia attention.'

We stopped at a room and Carol unlocked the door. 'The doors lock from the outside but the patients can open them from inside,' she said. 'Otherwise the wanderers, go into each other's rooms,' she added, seeing my puzzled expression.

I remembered Judy telling me about one of the patients when she'd worked there; they mustn't have had locks on the doors in those days. An old man kept going from room to room, pouring jugs of water over the beds. 'I'm watering the garden,' he'd explained.

The room we entered was bright and cheery. A single bed with a flowery bedspread was against one wall. There was a modern bedside table, small chest of drawers and a wardrobe; the room also contained an en-suite shower, sink and toilet.

A large window with similar flowery curtains overlooked an enclosed garden. 'That's where the ambulant patients can walk about and sit out in good weather. Relatives can introduce their own furnishings if they wish,' Carol said as we looked around the room. 'We advise them to bring things that hold memories, especially photographs. All the rooms will be done to this standard in time.'

We headed back downstairs and I was introduced to staff as we proceeded. They were mainly female, only a couple of men, all of varying ages. 'We always have qualified nursing staff on duty, one upstairs, one down, plus a number of care assistants who take examinations to increase their knowledge and qualifications. If your husband came in for respite care, we'd try to accommodate him downstairs. I'll show you the rooms.'

She showed me two more rooms, one small and newly furnished, plus a larger room, comfortable but timeworn with older, solid furniture. My first impressions of both the staff and the accommodation were very good; obviously the unit was geared for the needs of dementia patients. It was also a fully-equipped nursing home, which could deal with all the accompanying health and loss of mobility problems.

As we re-entered the main sitting room, I noticed patients sitting reading newspapers and magazines at the central table. Others were in chairs while staff chatted to them, going through photographs or books. 'We do everything we can to stimulate our residents,' said Carol, as a black-and-white cat walked past and jumped up onto a waiting knee. 'That's Felix. The residents love her and she's an amazingly gentle and friendly cat.'

We moved on into a smaller room, again with easy chairs; a large television filled one corner. A door led out into the enclosed garden. As we entered, two men came back in through the door, carefully watched by a nursing assistant. One resident came over and stood in a confrontational manner in front of Carol. 'It won't do, the engine fits this way,' he said, gesticulating dramatically with his hands. 'What do you know about it? I won't put up with it.'

Carol put an arm round his shoulders. 'Don't worry about it, Fred,' she said. 'We'll sort something out. It'll be lunchtime soon. It's beef stew today, your favourite.'

Fred pulled away but was a little calmer. 'He needs changing,' Carol added to the carer, glancing down at Fred's trousers. Fred was steered away to his room. At the same time someone started shouting, 'Martha are you there? Are you there, our Martha?' over and over, the same words in an agonised wail.

We headed back to the office where Judy was waiting. The cat was asleep, curled on an old man's knee; he smiled as he slowly worked his bony fingers through its fur. Around the room other patients nodded in various degrees of sleep, warm blankets tucked around their knees. Another was laughing as she shared a joke with a carer.

What was I thinking as I walked around? I felt a sense of having stepped into a different world. It was as if the real world existed through the double doors but in here was a place cut off from reality. I had no doubt that the care was excellent. I could understand that relatives would feel confident to trust their loved ones to the home – but surely Eddie had no place here?

Eddie wasn't this bad. Alright, he was confused, paranoid at times, but never as far gone into dementia as the majority of the people I had seen. Most were shadows of their former selves; they retained patchy memories, but were lost along this cruel pathway. If Eddie found it difficult to settle in the day-care centre, where the patients could still hold basic conversations, play games, do jigsaws, carry on in their own homes, how could he possibly fit in here? I shuddered at the prospect of him arriving into this extraordinary arena, surrounded by strangers behaving in bizarre ways. I just couldn't do it to him. No! No! my mind clamoured as I thanked Carol and we headed back to the car.

The next day, as Eddie's legs were a bit stronger, we went over to see his sister. He was fine, apart from the confusion. He spent most of the time reminiscing about the past. Their childhood days were very clear still, but he talked about Bobby and his parents as if they were still alive. I'd warned Ruby to play along with him but I could see how much it upset her.

I had two visits around this time, the first from Eden Carers. This is a local organisation which supports people who are caring for relatives at home for whatever reason. They offer advice as needed and have weekly get-togethers where carers can share problems and talk. He checked I had all the necessary nursing aids, and the available financial support.

'Come along to one of our meetings,' he said. 'We have a cup of tea and biscuits and a general social gathering. It does people good to talk about their situation, it makes you feel less alone.'

It all sounded fine but how could I leave Eddie? By now, I'd given up every activity I'd been involved in, even my WI. I could only go into town when Eddie was at day care, and only leave him alone if one of his friends or a neighbour could sit with him. I already felt that I was encroaching on people's goodwill; it was our problem and it was unfair to expect others to keep taking on the burden. Also, Eddie's confusion was becoming so erratic that it was increasingly difficult to ask anyone to stay with him for any length of time.

I took down the details and thanked him but had little hope of getting to any of the meetings.

The second visit was from the Home Care Department. It was a very nice lady who came to discuss the problem. She, like Nurse Maggie, suggested some home care, which I'd already considered but dismissed. The main problem was that if home carers came, as they did with my mother in her last year, they arrived at a set time. Usually they came in the morning to help the patient to get up, washed and dressed; if needed, they returned in the evening to put the patient back to bed. With Eddie's unpredictable condition and irregular habits, this type of home care was impossible.

She also suggested someone came on a regular day each week to sit with Eddie while I went out, and the possibility of that person taking Eddie out for a visit somewhere he might enjoy. Again it all sounded good but, having lived with the complications of dementia, I could see a number of pitfalls.

To begin with, Eddie was becoming increasingly suspicious of people he didn't know. How would he react to a stranger in his house? For the same reason, would he want to go anywhere with them? There was his inconsistent behaviour to factor in, the incontinence, plus his irregular mobility. It was agreed that she'd speak to her colleagues, get back to me and hopefully try to arrange something in the next couple of weeks.

November arrived. It was just over a year since Eddie had been diagnosed and we'd travelled a long way on the dementia journey since then. My carefully laid 'I can cope plan' was gradually unravelling as the days progressed.

The move downstairs had placed all the same problems on one level. I think I was now living on the edge of both a mental and physical breakdown brought on by months of short intervals of broken sleep, incessant worry and the daily strain of living hour by hour.

Eddie's niece, Bobby's daughter, arrived with Ruby to see us on 2nd November. She was up in the area from her home near London for a few days and she wanted to see Eddie, but also I'd asked her to help me fill in some forms granting me power of attorney. This was something that I'd been advised to sort out months before but I'd shied away from it. It meant that I'd have the power to deal with all financial and other decisions on Eddie's behalf.

When it had first been suggested, when Eddie would have understood, I'd felt very uncomfortable about explaining the implications to him. In the early stages of his illness, when we'd still been going to the bank together and sorting out everyday payments, how could I have expected him to sign a form handing the running of his life over to me? I could just imagine him saying, 'Do you think I'm going daft, Jackie?'

Now it was becoming more important that I had the power to deal with all aspects of his life as well as my own. I wondered if it were possible for Eddie to understand it's meaning or even sign his name, but a first step was to get the forms filled in so that's what we did.

During the week, the problems gathered pace. With growing difficulty we struggled on with day care. Eddie went reluctantly and I started arriving to pick him up around noon. Some days he could barely stand and transferring from wheelchair to taxi became more and more difficult. Add to this that I had to bring him home, get him out of the car and back into the chair and house alone.

Most days he accused me of wanting to kill him; either I had a gun or a knife tucked away. He became afraid and fought to get out of the house on legs which threatened to let him down at any moment while I rushed around with a chair, manoeuvring it behind him as he slumped backwards.

Each evening he still demanded to be 'taken home', and wouldn't rest until I gave in. Trying not to slip on the ice, I'd get the wheelchair to the car, heave him into the front seat and we'd set off. Round and round the village, over the moor, along lanes pressed into hard-packed snow by tyre treads.

I vividly remember one trip mainly because, in some strange way, Eddie was very clear-headed. It was just becoming twilight when he insisted we go. It was cold, still early evening, with a slight covering of snow on the fields. I backed down the yard and headed off down the back of the village.

'Turn left,' Eddie directed.

This took us onto a small back road and we drove for about a mile. It was a deep red sunset and the fields appeared pink as the dying strands of day bathed the snow. I went slowly, not just because of the road condition but hoping we'd soon be able to return home.

'This is it,' said Eddie, pointing to a small right hand turning that in all the years I'd lived in the village I'd hardly noticed and never travelled.

'Where does it go?' I asked, dreading we might end in a ploughed field.

'You'll see, just keep going.'

We ambled along a narrow tarmac lane, thankful that it had warmed during the daylight and removed the ice. There was a scattering of trees and bushes on either side, their bare winter branches standing black and stark against the pink-painted fields. A few sheep watched our slow progress with little interest, but we saw no people and passed no buildings.

'Me and Bobby used to come along here when we were lads,' said Eddie. He smiled as he spoke, a glistening of tears in his blue eyes. Did he remember for once that Bobby was no longer alive?

Darkness was almost upon us when we emerged at last onto the main road which led back to the village. Eddie laughed. 'See, this is where it comes out.' Yes, he'd remembered. 'Come on, our Jackie, let's go home,' he urged, as we headed back to the waiting lights and warmth.

Crisis point was reached on Wednesday 9th November. We'd had an awful night. Eddie wouldn't go to bed until after midnight, was up three or four times before 3am and never slept afterwards. That meant I didn't sleep either. I lost count of the number of times he wanted the commode and I managed to haul him out of bed and back again. His legs were really bad during the night and, when I eventually got him up at seven, he could just about step from bed to wheelchair. I helped him wash, shave and dress, into the front room via his wheelchair, finally transferring him into his electrically-powered chair for breakfast.

He was even more confused than normal and wanting the loo every twenty minutes, where he'd pass just a teaspoonful of urine. Did he have a urinary infection? I phoned the doctor. Could I send a specimen over? Charlie was at home in the bungalow, willingly took the specimen and returned with some medication.

A car drove past the house up to the field. Eddie managed to hoist himself out of his chair. 'We have to watch them, they're coming to steal the petrol,' he said, becoming agitated.

Someone came to the door and I answered it. When I returned, Eddie had tumbled onto the couch. 'Those people are here again. I don't know who the nosey buggers are. Go on! Get out!' he shouted, as I propped him up and got him back into his chair.

Nurse Maggie turned up late morning. Things were no

better. 'You'll have to get some home care in,' she urged. 'At the very least you need a hoist.'

We talked for an hour as Eddie kept trying to get up. 'I must be off and sort out those cows, they need milking.'

Between us we tried to reassure him that someone had already been to milk and that he needn't worry. He was calmer when she left with a promise that she'd be back the next day. 'Phone if you need someone in between.'

We got through lunchtime as I ticked off the hours. One bad hour, one good. Eddie's legs were stronger as the afternoon came. He was still wanting the commode every half hour but at least he could stand to pass water.

Around 2pm, he insisted he must check on the cows. Terrified he'd tumble, I tried to stop him but he brushed me aside. 'They've got to be fed.'

He was adamant, so into coat and Wellingtons and off we went down to the redundant cowshed. He had his stick in one hand, me hanging onto the other. Somehow we made it back and forth without him ending up on the ground; the return lap was managed by him holding onto the garden wall then the house for support. I sighed with relief when we gained the safety of the house.

Rachel, the social worker, arrived at 4pm. She'd been coming every month then every two weeks; I now felt towards her as I did with Nurse Maggie, that she was both professional help and a friend. It was a coincidence that she was due the same day as Maggie, but I think that the nurse must have phoned her after she'd seen us that morning.

The rolling snowball had now gained the size and momentum of a boulder. I'd already had an uncontrollable howl all over Maggie and, as I opened the door to Rachel, I burst into tears once more. Looking back as I write, I feel both ashamed and useless that I was unable to hold the floodgates in check any longer. I was adrift, lost in this welter of emotion, feeling a weak fool, unable to contain my feelings.

Who was I crying for? Eddie: yes, I was crying for Eddie. I wanted him back. Not the muddled-up man I'd been caring for but the laughing, funny, kind and generous human being that I loved. I wanted to go back to those wonderful holidays, lying in the sunshine on the cruises and exploring all those amazing places we'd visited. Was I crying for myself? Yes: I was tired beyond expression but I was also so sad, sunk into this well of despair.

We walked through into the living room where Eddie was watching the television. As we came in, he started to struggle out of his chair. 'I need the loo,' he said. I rushed for the commode while Rachel operated the button which raised the chair upright. He squirted out his teaspoon of urine. I sorted out his pad and string pants and settled him once more. 'We must go and check on those cows,' he said.

Rachel sat with him, trying to make him understand that he needn't bother with the cows as we had someone looking after them while he wasn't well. As she talked, I stood at the back of the room, the tears running like a river down my cheeks.

'Eddie must go in for respite care,' she said. 'If you don't give in, it'll be you in hospital.' I tried to argue through the tears. 'No, this time I'm going to insist for both your sakes. Judy took you round Silverdown. Would you be prepared to let Eddie go there?'

I was unable to speak; I just nodded. Truly, at that moment I wished both of us were dead. He wouldn't have to go away from his home into that unknown, frightening place, and I wouldn't have to worry and cry any longer. I was beyond logic, beyond systematic thought. I was being sucked down into some void of desperation, some bottomless pit of distress.

'Two weeks,' she said. 'Two weeks and see how things are.'

'No, one week,' I sobbed.

'Two weeks. Come on, I've got the number. Make the phone call.'

'I can't!' I howled. Inside I was screaming. 'No! No!'

'Then I'll phone,' she said, walking past me to pick up the receiver.

I sobbed the whole time she was on the phone, soaking a handkerchief, wrapped in this shroud of inconsolable grief.

Eddie was still watching the television; there was a programme on about horses, which he enjoyed. When he looked at us, he smiled in a puzzled way, his eyes saying, 'Why's she upset?'

I was shaking by the time Rachel finished the phone call. 'Two people from Silverdown will come to assess Eddie this evening. They'll have a chat with you both, but it's merely a formality. They have an emergency respite room available and Eddie can go tomorrow morning.'

So that was it: the decision was made and I just couldn't fight any longer. I had no idea how I was going to explain to Eddie where he was going. At that moment I was existing on automatic pilot, trying not to think about tomorrow, trying not to think about how he would react to Silverdown.

I phoned Charlie, who was at home in the bungalow for a few days, crying as usual as I told him what had happened. 'Will you drive us?' I asked. I knew I'd be in no state to face both taking Eddie away and the road. It was agreed that Charlie would bring the car round the next morning as soon as we were ready. Rachel had said there was no fixed time to take Eddie in so I could get him up and dressed without any rush. There was still the Silverdown care assessment that evening but, unlike Sunnygarth, this time it really was going to happen.

They arrived at 7pm. One of them was Carol, the manager whom I'd met on my visit with Judy; the other was one of the male care workers – I'll call him Bruce. I was trembling as I let them in and we went through into the living room. They relaxed into armchairs and I put the kettle on as they chatted to Eddie, who was still confused but calm. He hadn't a clue who they were, and I'd said nothing about them coming.

'How you doing, Eddie?' Carol asked, as Eddie smiled and assured them he was fine. 'What do you like to do, Eddie, when you're not working?'

'Well, the cows take up a lot of time, you know. There's the milking and mucking out. Hard work, especially this time of the year.'

'There's not much spare time on a farm, is there?' Carol agreed. 'How many cows have you?'

Eddie considered. 'Twenty-five,' he said. 'And a few calves. But we only have a smallholding, so it's what you call a flying herd.' They laughed as Eddie continued, obviously very much at ease with them. 'We buy heifers in as needed and only keep the calves for a few weeks. Not enough acreage to breed our own.' It was strange how Eddie got his facts correct as he chatted; the only drawback was that he talked as if his farming life was unaltered and had not been abandoned some years before.

'How long have you been farming?' Carol asked.

'Since I left school. I could have gone on to grammar but money was short in those days, so me brother went and I stayed working on the farm.'

As they talked, I tried to grasp the strange see-saw symptoms of dementia. Anyone listening, not knowing the facts, would think it was merely an elderly farmer, chatting quite normally about his farm. The truth – that he was existing in a parallel life – would surprise them.

'So what else do you enjoy besides the farm?'

'I like horses.' Eddie thought for a few seconds. 'I used to go each year to the TT races in the Isle of Man when I was younger. And I read the paper each day.'

'Which paper do you read?'

'Daily Mail, and the Herald – oh, and the farming papers.'

'Let's have a look at how you're walking now. You've been having a bit of bother recently,' said Carol, as she and Bruce helped Eddie up.

'His legs are unpredictable. Some days they're really good, other days he can hardly manage a step,' I said, trying to keep calm.

'No problem,' said Carol, as they settled Eddie back into his chair. 'What do you like to eat, Eddie?'

'Oh, most things. I like rice pudding, and custard, and I always have porridge in a morning.'

'We can manage that okay.'

'He only wears his top set of teeth, so he's not good with anything that's hard or needs a lot of chewing,' I pointed out.

'I bet you like cottage pie, with some peas and nice gravy.'

'I don't like carrots.'

'Would you like to come and stay with us for a while, Eddie?' Carol asked.

I waited for him to say no, to ask if I was coming as well or just bluntly refuse, but strangely he didn't. He just nodded. I wondered if he'd heard what was said or understood their meaning.

They continued to chat as I gave out cups of tea. I stood behind Eddie's chair so he couldn't see I was blubbing again. What was I thinking as the conversation went on? My mind was swirling, thinking back to my Silverdown visit and remembering my impressions on that day. How could I let Eddie go somewhere like that? What would he think of me? How could I do that to this wonderful, caring man? Would he have abandoned me? Never.

The more I churned the thoughts round and round, the more those inevitable tears came and I had to walk away so Eddie wouldn't see and hear me sobbing.

Carol came over to me, placing a comforting arm on mine. 'Don't worry, he'll be fine. We'll take good care of him. You'll be surprised how well he'll settle. Most of our patients do and it's obvious that Eddie is, by character, a happy, contented chap.'

I had my doubts but the decision was made, and I knew I had no option.

'Take your time. Come when you're ready tomorrow. His room will be ready.'

'What do I need to bring?' I asked.

'Clothes for a couple of weeks, basics like washing and shaving stuff. Bring some items that hold memories for him, perhaps a wedding photo – whatever you think Eddie will enjoy having in his room. You needn't worry about pads and towels, we provide all that sort of thing.'

They stayed for an hour before driving away, leaving me feeling as if I was wading through an impenetrable bog of emotion.

The remainder of the evening passed uneventfully, apart from me slipping away to pack him a case. I'd decided I would wait until the morning before telling him he was going away for a few days. He'd already forgotten about the visit of the Silverdown staff.

The treatment for his urinary infection was taking effect, so he wasn't wanting to pass water as often. This was a point in his deterioration when he was incontinent but at times knew he wanted the loo. He could demand the toilet, pass nothing and then fill his pad ten minutes later. At other times he went without trouble.

We had our usual restless night, up around six times, me changing the bed once in the middle of the night. Eddie slept fitfully; I tossed, turned, worried and wept. I gave up about 8.30 and got up, but Eddie was deeply asleep. I decided not to wake him but get him up when he was ready.

It was 9.45 when he stirred and, with difficulty, I got him out of bed and onto the commode. His legs were really bad that morning. I shaved and washed him, making bits of conversation, but he was quieter than usual. Had he remembered? I managed to get him to put on his trousers and stand him up for a few seconds while I pulled them up, then got him sorted with a newly laundered shirt and jumper. I wanted him to look nice.

He managed to comb his hair; such a chap he was for his comb. The times I remember him saying, 'The wind's blown my hair, I'll have to comb it,' or 'I can't change my jumper, I've just combed my hair.' He still had a thick covering of blond-silver hair, even though he was in his late seventies. His main worry when he'd had to have his brain operation was, 'Will they shave my head? I don't want them to shave off my hair.' I remember running my fingers through his hair. These thoughts were tumbling round my mind.

We'd been progressing fine, if slowly, but then I had to transfer him to his wheelchair to move him through to the front room. I managed to haul him up as his legs wobbled and I tried to swing him gently across to the chair, but it was no good; he overbalanced and slid to the carpet. He didn't hurt himself – it wasn't a fall, more a slither – but once on the carpet, there was no way I could get him up. I knew I'd have to get help so, wrapping him in a blanket to keep him warm, I phoned Arty.

God bless him! He came straight round. 'Come on, Eddie,' he said. 'Let's have you up.' They were old friends and I could see Arty was moved to see this once-strong, energetic farmer so helpless. He lifted him easily into the wheelchair and helped me push him through to the front room. 'Give me a ring when you're ready to go and I'll come and lift him into the car.'

I decided to leave Eddie in the chair for his breakfast and not sit him at the table as usual. He was becoming more confused again.

'Are you going to have your porridge?' I asked, holding the bowl for him. He made no effort to eat so I placed a towel under his chin and started slowly spooning the porridge.

He took a few mouthfuls before his eyes watered. 'Where's Mam? I want my mam,' he cried. 'Please, where's Mam?'

I'd never known him say this before; for a while he became the little boy he'd once been, searching desperately for the mother he loved and depended on. I tried to comfort him but at that moment I was a poor substitute.

It was approaching 11am by the time all was ready. I phoned Charlie to bring round the car, and Arty. It was a cold but dry morning. I'd managed to get Eddie into one of his thick, woolly, outdoor jackets that he wore around the farm. Afterwards he was quiet, gently dozing in his wheelchair.

'You're going on a little journey,' I told him when everyone was assembled.

We pushed the chair out through the side door to Charlie's car.

'Come on, Eddie! Up you come,' said Arty, helping him to stand and taking his weight as he lowered him into the front seat of Charlie's car.

Eddie seemed dazed, as if the world were flowing by him, but he was just an observer. Was it the effects of the urinary infection, a particularly bad morning or were we gradually taking another step along our journey?

I was holding on, trying not to think, trying to detach myself from this impending event. I felt as if I were floating on a sea of unreality; none of this could be happening. Ever since the doctor had pronounced those words 'vascular dementia', I'd found it difficult to believe any of this was possible.

Eddie was this sturdy, hard-working man who could go for ten years without seeing a doctor. He ailed little, apart from the odd cold or bout of flu, and his blood pressure and angina problems had produced little cause for concern over the years. He was sound and solid, like a reliable oak. He was as much a part of the land as the grass it grew and the stock that grazed.

I thanked Arty. Charlie started the car and we drove out of the yard, out of the village and over the moor. I was in the back seat, a hand resting on Eddie's shoulder. Charlie and I chatted to him; he made little response but slept most of the way. I remember little of the trip as the well-known landmarks slipped by. Somehow I held onto my self-control. I was determined that today, for Eddie's sake, I must be brave.

We drove along the A6 for twenty minutes before turning down the lane to Silverdown, a further mile. A mile seems a short distance when written down but this mile was an eternity for me. It was a major stride along our journey, a giant step into the unknown. This mile had started way back on the cruise, when Eddie had asked if the car was parked outside; most likely it had started long before, when I wasn't even aware we had begun the journey. This was a mile that I had never expected or believed we would ever have to travel.

For the second time I was in a car that crunched over gravel as we turned into the drive of Silverdown Care Home. Charlie stopped. I climbed out and went to inform the staff we'd arrived. Back into the vestibule, sign the book, press the intercom – but this time I was bringing Eddie.

The door was soon opened and a couple of carers came with a wheelchair to transfer Eddie from the car. He appeared indifferent to the situation as he was pushed into the unfamiliar surroundings. Charlie and I followed, me clutching his case. We passed through the main sitting room and turned left down a corridor. 'Eddie's room's down here,' said the carer.

We arrived at a brown door, a key was turned and we passed into a spacious, if rather dark, room. It was one of those still awaiting upgrading. It contained a single bed pushed up against one wall, a side table, a large, old-fashioned wardrobe, a dressing table with mirror, a round wooden table and an easy chair.

'You okay, Eddie?' the carers asked. 'He does like to be called Eddie?' they checked with me. I nodded. 'I'll bring you two chairs and a tray of tea and biscuits.'

Eddie sat quietly in the wheelchair, seemingly oblivious to his change of surroundings. The chairs and tea arrived and we settled around the table, making conversation.

'It's a nice big room,' said Charlie. 'Care-home rooms are usually very cramped. You okay, Eddie?' he asked in his Scottish accent.

Eddie gave no reply. Was he asleep, I wondered?

'Do you want a drink, love?' I asked.

There was a slight shaking of his head then he lolled in the chair, his breathing coming in quick, noisy gasps. Alarmed, I sprang up. God! Had he suffered a stroke with the upset of the move? I rushed off to get a nurse. She came rapidly and tested his pulse. 'Eddie! Eddie! Can you hear me?' she urged, trying to stir him, but for the moment he was very still, his breathing almost non-existent.

I stood at his side like a statue, wondering for a few seconds if he'd died. Charlie and I exchanged anxious looks. The nurse tried again to stir him, her fingers on his pulse. Then after a minute – though it felt longer – Eddie moaned. He moved, his eyes opened and he yawned.

'He had a short black-out,' said the nurse. 'I'll come back and take his blood pressure.'

It was agreed it would be better if he had a sleep in bed and two carers arrived to sort him out. As I handed over his case, I wondered if I should stay. I gave him a kiss but he made little response; he was already asleep.

'Don't worry, we'll make him comfortable. He'll be alright,' said one of the carers.

I don't remember walking out of his room; I think Charlie had hold of me.

The nurse was waiting. 'He'll be okay. I think he's just tired and his blood pressure was a little low. His pulse is strong and he's breathing normally. If it happens again, we'll send for the doctor. Phone up any time to enquire, and you know you can come whenever you want to see him.' She could see the state I was in and a comforting arm came around my shoulders. 'You've done the right thing. Try not to worry.'

Charlie steered me to the main door, the nurse entered the code and we were back outside in the cold, crunching back to the car over the chippings.

I have little memory of the journey back apart from crying the whole way.

CHAPTER 7

'THE MOST TERRIBLE DECISION OF MY LIFE'

Two weeks, fourteen days, 336 hours.

The house felt bereft when I returned home. Lost, I wandered around. I made tea; it went cold. I switched on the television; it babbled on unheard as I sat oblivious. I stoked the Rayburn, stripped Eddie's bed and put in a wash, all without real thought. It was only when my black cat, Alfie, clambered onto my knee that I started to cry again. Rocking back and forth, burying my face in his fur.

I phoned the home at around 3.30. 'Don't worry, he's fine,' they assured me. 'He's had a sleep and he's back up, and sitting having his afternoon tea. We'll tell him you called.'

Partly pacified, I tried to settle but my mind wasn't at rest. I was at Silverdown, worrying. I'd told the staff a lot about Eddie, about his behaviour, night-time restlessness, unstable mobility, but they had other patients to look after. I'd only had him. Would he be alright by himself in his bedroom at night? What if he got out of bed with no one watching him? What if he fell? Would he start fretting, as he had at the day-care centre? Would he start to panic because I wasn't there? I just churned around from one worry to another.

Maggie phoned early evening to ask how I was. I just about managed to hold a conversation.

'Take time for yourself,' she advised. 'You'll be able to catch up on some sleep. If I were you, I wouldn't go and see Eddie tomorrow. Wait until Saturday.'

I started to protest: no, I must go. Every nerve screamed to see him; part of me wanted to jump into the car that moment and belt off back to Silverdown.

'If you go tomorrow, you'll possibly do more harm than good. Let him settle and give yourself time to calm down.'

I knew she was right; if I went tomorrow, I would be going for myself more than for Eddie and I might make matters worse. Maggie assured me that the home would phone if I was required.

By bedtime I felt both physically and mentally exhausted. There had been no further phone calls. I went into the downstairs bedroom; Eddie's bed looked so lonely, so empty. Sleepless, I turned over and over in bed. I put the light back on and tried to read but the words made no impression. After reading the same sentence four times, I gave up.

I got out of bed and padded off to the kitchen, made a drink of hot chocolate and watched the television as the clock ticked to 2am then 3am. Was Eddie asleep? Was he warm enough? Was he afraid?

Back to bed. I must have fallen asleep; the next thing I knew it was morning and a cold wintery light was peeping through a gap in the curtains. The phone, which I kept at my bedside, had remained silent. Both Eddie and I had got through the night.

Reluctantly, I had resolved to follow Maggie's advice and not visit Eddie that day. I'd been warned that there wasn't always someone around to answer the telephone but I got through at 10am.

'He's had a good night, been up a few times but no problems. He had a good breakfast, porridge and toast just like home, and he's sitting in the day room, chatting to the staff.'

Relieved, I thanked them, told them to telephone my home number or mobile if they needed to contact me and said I'd be in the next day.

I have found throughout life that, no matter what disasters or upsets we encounter, it is impossible to be sad all the time. I think by that morning, at least for the time being, I was 'cried out'.

I actually had plans for that day. The bookshop in Carnforth was stocking my first book, Cats Like Me, and they wanted me to go over and do a book signing. I'd intended either to take Eddie with me or have a friend come and watch him for a few hours. Now, for the first time in months, I was free to go somewhere without complicated arrangements and worry.

I tried not to think about Eddie as I drove to Carnforth and enjoyed the two hours at the shop. We only sold four books but I had a good chat to the customers and staff. I'd intended to come straight home but realised there was no rush. It was one of those cold, fine November days, so I decided to go to the famous Carnforth Station.

You have to be of a certain age or love old films to remember Brief Encounter with Trevor Howard and Celia Johnson. They don't make them like that anymore. I'd been with Eddie a number of years before when they had reopened the station but now there was much more going on. There was a shop and exhibition area, plus a good café with a delicious-sounding menu.

I decided to have lunch then a wander around. As I was waiting, the people around me surged out onto the platform. I followed, wondering what was happening. To the sound of a whistle and billowing smoke, a steam train chugged in and drew up at the platform. Some passengers got on, others waved from the windows. How the train brought back memories of my childhood when we went on our annual holidays to Welshpool.

We'd leave Ashton-under-Lyne at the crack of dawn and walk to Charleston Station, my dad toting two large cases. Onto the Manchester train, then on to Crewe before our final change for Wales. We'd climb aboard and make ourselves comfy, hoping to have the carriage to ourselves. I remember the train doors, the window straps and that exciting 'clickety-click, clickety-click'.

The whistle shrilled again, more smoke, and the old steam train chugged away to a cheer, rapidly disappearing down the line. It was a real bonus to my visit.

I decided to go mid-morning the next day to see Eddie. As my car drew into the car park I was shaking, wondering what was waiting for me behind the locked doors. I'd brought him a newspaper but nothing else, deciding I'd assess his needs when I saw him.

I crunched over the white gravel path, opened the outer door and signed the visitors' book. I had to put my name, car registration, time of arrival and who I was visiting. It was strange but this was the only time in my life that I remembered my car number. I recall Eddie and I going to Skipton and joining a long queue to pay the required parking fee, only to have to dash back to the car as I had to input my car number and I hadn't a clue what it was. I've always had a blank when it comes to numbers but I was to write this number down so often when I visited Eddie that it felt like it was stamped on my psyche.

That done, I sanitised my hands and pressed the request-for-admission button. A disembodied voice answered and I said, 'It's Jackie Huck, come to see Eddie.'

One of the staff arrived rapidly and opened the door. I was greeted by a smile as she introduced herself. I found that gradually I came to know the staff well. 'He's sitting in the day room, having morning coffee,' she said. 'Would you like a drink?' I said yes as she ushered me in. 'He's just over there,' she said, pointing.

He was dressed and sitting in one of the easy chairs which hugged three walls. His hair was obviously freshly combed and he'd been shaved. A green blanket covered his knees and a small table stood nearby, where his cup of coffee was within easy reach accompanied by a small plate of biscuits.

His face lit up as he saw me but with delight, not worry or anxiety. 'Oh, you've got the paper,' he said. 'I've been looking round the house for it but I thought it hadn't come.'

I pulled up a chair so I was sitting near.

'Do you want a biscuit?' he asked, pushing the plate towards me. 'There's a chocolate, your favourite.'

My cup of tea arrived. I thanked the carer and nibbled a biscuit. 'How are you?'

'Oh, I'm fine. A bit tired. I've been busy since I got up. The cows pushed down a wall up the top field, made a right mess. I've been up there sorting it. I'll go back after I've had me break.'

I drifted as he rambled, content in his made-up world. I realised, in some ways with relief, that he had no idea where he was. As far as he was concerned, he was carrying on his life as usual.

'I went to Carnforth yesterday,' I told him. 'I sold a few books then went onto the station. A steam train came through. There were a lot of people around.'

'Have you got a ticket?' he asked. One of the carers walked past collecting empty cups. 'I think she's selling tickets. You better get one before the ticket inspector comes round. I don't want them chucking you off the train.' He beckoned her over, handing her his cup. 'The wife needs a ticket,' he said.

She smiled. 'Don't worry, I'll get her one.'

'There's a lot of people waiting on the station today,' he carried on. 'Where they all going?'

'Oh, I expect they're off to lots of places – Carlisle, Newcastle, perhaps as far as London.'

A tall man in a striped jumper walked over and stood over us, his fists balled. 'It's important. It must be connected right, otherwise it won't work. Have you got the wire?' His face screwed up with anger. 'Are you listening? How can you expect it to work? The connection's broken. This has to connect to that.' He worked his hands in the air, fastening and joining invisible strands, his anger and frustration growing. I noticed his trousers were wet where the urine had seeped through.

Eddie didn't seem to notice; I was incapable of speech. A carer appeared. 'Come on, Sam. How about we get you changed? It'll be dinner soon. It's chips today.' He let them lead him away.

'He's a grand chap, is that,' said Eddie. 'He's the engine driver.'

I stayed for nearly two hours. We went from the railway station to Australia as I mentioned my friend Pauline had gone there to visit her son.

'Oh, our Ruby's been there for years,' Eddie nodded. 'She likes it but says it's very hot. I don't like it too hot. We'll have to get sun hats before we go out walking.' I agreed as he continued, 'Our Bobby's out here as well but he's not sure whether he'll stay. When do we go home?'

'Soon,' I assured him.

'Oh, that's good but I don't want to fly. Can we go home

by ship? I like those big ships.'

I was now deep inside his world as we talked about our time at sea and the four cruises we'd enjoyed during the last few years. Eddie laughed as he remembered; yes, he did remember but, like the jumble of his mind, he remembered in a distorted way. 'We'll have a walk along the sun deck,' he said.

'And afternoon tea around the pool. We can have some of those fancy sandwiches and dainty little cakes, and trifle for afters.'

'We can't take too long, though,' he said. 'I'll have to see to the cows before it gets dark.' He broke off and looked around, but what was he seeing? 'Oh, here comes the captain,' he said, as one of the care workers walked by. 'We shook hands with him last night and had our pictures taken.'

As the minutes ticked away, I realised that I was running out of control. I knew I must be brave and hold on to this great swell of emotion that threatened to overpower me. Eddie was content, floating around in his imaginary world.

'Do you want to stop and have lunch with Eddie?' one of the carers asked.

'No, I think I'll go. I'll be back tomorrow.'

'Fine. But any time you want to stay, just say.'

I stood up, wondering how I could slip away and if he would miss me. 'Are you going ashore?' he asked.

'Yes, I just want a few souvenirs.'

'That's grand. I'll stay here round the pool. I might have a doze. You have a good time.'

I pushed my chair back, collected my coat and headed to the door, which was opened for me with the code number. I signed the book, noting the time I'd left, and drifted out into the cold winter's day. I was feeling weak and heady, my legs like rubber. Reaching the car, I sank into the driver's seat.

I drove away, my mind on automatic, the car wheels crunching over the white gravel surface. Down the road heading for the A6, I saw a layby and pulled in, where at last I broke down. I don't know how long I sat there, tears streaming down my face, my whole body wracked with sobs. I think I cried that day until I could cry no more; my head and neck ached with the effort. At last I felt I was safe enough to drive back through the villages, over the moor and eventually home. I was so exhausted, I collapsed onto the couch and slept for two hours.

It was only when I woke, brewed tea and had something to eat that I managed to think back and assess the situation. A few things were obvious. Eddie was not distressed by Silverdown, as I had expected. The surroundings and patients were more alien than the day-care centre, where only a few weeks before he'd felt threatened and called the patients daft. Now he accepted both an unfamiliar environment and advanced dementia patients. He saw what he wanted to see, conjured a world around himself, and was basically happy. Also, he didn't notice my absence. He had taken yet another step on the journey but I was left behind and could not follow.

I was now presented with another painful truth: Eddie was being better looked after by the staff than by me. I was a weak, tired woman, exhausted by worry and lack of sleep and without the strength to physically lift him when it was needed.

Was love enough? Eddie was due back home in twelve days. Would I be able to cope when he returned? Even though I would have had a rest, how long before I was again drained of energy? For the moment, he appeared more comfortable and contented at Silverdown than he'd been at home. I felt sick as, for the first time, the thought entered my mind that perhaps for his sake he was better off there.

To my shame, I recalled in the past being at times judgemental when I'd heard that someone's husband or wife had been placed in a care home, especially when the partner seemed able bodied. Surely that was part of the deal: 'in sickness and in health' and 'til death do us part'. How awful, I would think, to just dump someone into a care home and carry on with your life. I never gave much thought to the circumstances, the path they must have trod to reach that decision. Now here I was, on the edge of this terrible abyss, daring to think the unthinkable.

I went most days to see Eddie. I found the best time to go was mid-morning and to leave when he was getting ready for his lunch; it was a good time to slip away un-noticed. A few times I did stay and eat with him to give me an idea of what he was having and if he was eating. The food was plentiful and well cooked. Nothing too fancy, but that age group were used to basic good food and that's what they received. There was always a substantial main course, including cottage pie, meat and vegetables (in Eddie's case, the meat well cut up), fish and chips and occasionally a curry (not too spicy); dessert was rice pudding, some sort of crumble or pie with custard, or ice cream and jelly. If I stopped, a special table would be set aside in the dining room for us. It was comforting to see that Eddie was eating well.

One day at lunchtime he was asleep and refused to be roused. 'Don't worry,' I was assured. 'We'll keep it and give it to him as soon as he wakes.'

Around a week into his stay I had a long talk with Carol. 'What's he like during the night?' I asked, thinking about our nightly disturbances.

She reached for Eddie's folder where everything was recorded. 'He gets up now and again and has a wander. He's watched to make sure he doesn't fall. The staff change the bed as needed. During the night Eddie can either stay in the day room and have a drink or sleep or, if he wishes, they put him back into bed. There's no set rules. We let the patients do what they wish whenever possible.'

This was the difference. At home, because Eddie was doing what he wanted or whatever his dementia dictated, my sleep was disrupted night after night. Here the night staff took it all in their stride as part of their duties. They could sleep during the day.

'Has he had any strange psychotic attacks?' I asked. 'He was having them regularly at home, believing I was going to poison or knife him.'

Carol consulted the folder. 'He got very frightened the other evening but I was still on duty, and I sat with him and chatted. He soon calmed down. Another occasion he was convinced the building was on fire but we talked to him and gave him some ice cream, and he forgot about it.' She regarded me with understanding. 'When a patient comes here, they quite often have a change of behaviour. Some become much calmer, with others there's little change, but we are equipped and trained to deal with whatever happens. Have you given any thought to what you are going to do when the two weeks are up?'

Had I given any thought? I'd been thinking of little else! This had been a time for me to catch up on sleep but, if anything, I was sleeping even less and only when I was exhausted. I'd been lying in bed at that awful 2am time, going backwards and forwards over the problem, mulling and pondering. During the day I'd been cleaning up, preparing for his return, the house feeling hollow as if his unseen echo lingered. I would be looking forward to his return then suddenly reality would loom. How would I cope? Could I cope?

'What's his mobility been like?' I asked.

'It's different each day.'

I nodded; that had been my experience.

'The urinary infection has cleared, so that's helping. Some days he's a bit tottery and we either walk with him, or watch him carefully. Other days he walks around quite well. Of course,' Carol added, 'his mobility will become much worse. It's only a matter of time.'

'I'm almost certain that I'm going to take him home,' I said. This had to be the right decision; there was no way my beloved Eddie was going into a home permanently.

'Why did he come in?' Carol probed.

I felt those damn tears threatening again. 'It was all becoming too much,' I choked. 'Between the getting up time and again during the night, and the constant confusion during the day and the really bad psychotic incidents.' I rummaged in my handbag for a hanky. Why did I keep crying? Did I really have no self-control?

'Is it going to be any different if he goes home?'

'I'll be rested. I'll be able to manage better.'

'For how long?' she asked.

'Oh God,' I thought, 'for how long would I be able to manage?'

'Should you decide to admit Eddie as a resident, the room he's in at the moment is available, I know it's not been renovated yet but he seems happy in there.' The words hung in the air as I took deep breaths. 'We don't always have vacancies and once a room is occupied it can be a while before there's another place.' In other words, after a present resident has died. 'Anyway,' she continued, 'you've a week yet. I'll leave you to think it over.'

Most people in my situation would have consulted family,

assessed the opinion of sons and daughters, perhaps a sister or brother, but I had no family on my side to consult. I did talk on the phone to Eddie's sister, but she was still recovering from her illness and I didn't want to burden her with any share in my decision. That was the bare and uncomfortable truth: this had to be my decision, no one else's.

Over the next week, I talked to friends, not really to ask their advice more to chat and tell them how Eddie was getting on. I told them what Silverdown was like, about the staff, what a homely atmosphere they had created. I couldn't really describe the 'other world' feeling that descended the moment I walked through the door; that had to be experienced.

One friend did ask, 'Do you think he's better off there than at home?'

I remember feeling defensive, stressing this was only for a couple of weeks; he was coming home. I was fine now I'd had a rest; it was never intended to be permanent. She smiled as she pushed tea and biscuits in my direction. 'Are you being practical?' she asked. 'If you're not careful, it's going to be you who's the invalid then he'll have to go into a home – and perhaps not one of your choice.'

Another friend came with me on one of my visits. We signed in and were soon sitting with Eddie. The 'wanderers' ambled back and forth. I was becoming used to this confluence of troubled humanity, adrift in their broken minds. Shouts of 'Henry! Are you there Henry?' came from the small sitting room. Sam walked passed thumping the air in anger; Maisie sat buttoning and unbuttoning her cardigan, swearing the whole time.

I don't know what my friend thought; perhaps it was easier for her not being emotionally involved, but she might have been merely putting on a brave front for my benefit. The only one who seemed oblivious to it all was Eddie. He smiled and chatted about all the farm work he'd done that morning. 'I'm going to work on the tractor this afternoon,' he said. 'I think there's a bit of muck got into the tank. I'm going to drain it.'

We both played along, asking him about the farm, talking about the cows and the weather not being good for the hay. A tray of tea and biscuits had been brought to us. We tried not to notice our surroundings but pretend everything was normal and we were sharing a morning's 'crack' with a busy farmer.

I sobbed on her shoulder as we headed back to the car.

'He's happy and well looked after,' she said. 'He doesn't know what's happened. It's you who's doing the suffering.' I calmed down and we talked on the way home. 'When is he due to come home?' she asked.

'Wednesday.'

'What are you going to do?'

'I don't know, I can't decide.'

'You need to think of what's the best outcome for him, as well as yourself,' she advised.

'I can't take him out of his home permanently,' I said. 'He's the last person in the village living in the house where he was born. He's been there for seventy-nine years. I know he would have wanted to stay there until he died.'

'Jackie, he thinks he's still there.'

The days ticked away and, like the pendulum on the clock, I swung first one way and then the other. I found myself drifting round the house, sorting through his clothes, holding them like comfort blankets, taking in his smell. His neglected overalls and boots stood waiting; they seemed to sit in judgement, their presence a condemnation of my failure.

A short conversation I'd had with Bruce, the male carer who'd come to the house that evening with Carol, haunted me. 'He's a lovely man,' he'd said one day when I was visiting. 'He's always smiling. He must have been a good husband.'

I said he was the best but I wasn't sure if I could manage if I took him home. Bruce looked troubled. 'But you will take him home, won't you?'

This brought me to one swing of the pendulum – of course he's coming home. I would ask for extra help in the house, try the night-time sitter that had been suggested, let home carers come to get him up and dressed, perhaps others to help in an evening. Did I need a hoist? Perhaps that would help. And they did do day care at Silverdown; he could go twice a week. Yes: this would work, he would come home!

Then, just as swiftly, I swung in the other direction. He often went to bed any time of day then was up again. What about all the times he was up during the night? How could carers help with these problems? What if he had more psychotic attacks: how would I cope if he became angry and afraid, or even violent? This wasn't Eddie; when he was like this he became a stranger with no understanding or knowledge of what he was doing. He wouldn't be reasoned with. I'd already had to deal with these heart-rending attacks. I saw us again struggling in the hallway, him hammering on the glass door with his shoe trying to escape from me.

Yes, he could go to Silverdown for day care, but what if it unsettled him as it had when he'd gone to Appleby? At the moment he was settled and happy, cocooned in imaginary contentment. If I now disrupted him, brought him home then shipped him off twice a week, how would he react?

Then there was his mobility. In Silverdown, if needed, there were many hands to lift and steady him when he walked. Should he tumble, they could easily pick him up. At home there was just me, a wheelchair and a useless walking stick. I pictured us stumbling back and forwards around the house, to and from the car when we were off on one of his 'going home' sessions. Would this persist if he came home? He hadn't had any of these fantasies while he'd been away. Would they return if he came back?

I tried to analyse why he was always so convinced he wasn't at home. All I could deduce was that he was searching for his childhood home, looking around expecting to see the rooms as they were when he was a boy. The old kitchen, his mother at the range. I know Eddie did a lot of renovation before we married and we'd done a small amount afterwards, so to his confused mind he wasn't 'home'. But why wasn't he still searching at Silverdown? Either he was now seeing what he wanted as his dementia advanced, or, with the surroundings being totally alien, his mind had somehow accepted the change. I didn't know but I dreaded going back to the nightmare our lives had become.

On some unknown ship we sailed,
the tide is always out
awash with doubt,
there is no path across the waves
to save, only a far horizon,
which slips further away
day by day.

Lost in shifting currents,
adrift upon a lonely crest,
neither east nor west
but somewhere in between.
Unseen our ship sails on,
gone into some void of no return.

Thursday 24th November 2011 loomed, the day Eddie's

two weeks respite care was over and he must either come home or be admitted. I had to let them know on Wednesday so they knew whether to release the room the following day.

Tuesday was the worst night of my life. Weighed down by indecision, my head throbbed and I ached from crying. Yes – more tears; perhaps they were a safety valve, perhaps without this persistent outlet of emotion I would have collapsed.

I paced the house, room by room. I opened the wardrobe where his clothes hung, his many shirts and jumpers – just a few had been taken to Silverdown for his short stay. I sorted through his sock drawer, ran my fingers through his ties. Eddie loved his ties; he had a large selection which had been added to because of our holidays. There was his tartan one, bought in a clan shop in Scotland, and his special Oriana tie bought on our first cruise.

I hugged his jumpers, burying my face in the thick wool. These had gone under his overalls to keep him warm around the farm on the many winter days he had worked the land. He had both heavy and light nylon overalls, which he wore depending on the season. He had a large pile that occupied a sizable area in the airing cupboard. I liked him to have a clean one each day. Some farmers wore the same one for days and the wretched things could almost stand up by themselves.

In the spare-room wardrobe hung his special suits, jackets and shirts, which he wore on the cruises. I remembered getting ready for that first cruise, going into a gentlemen's outfitters in town to buy Eddie his dress suit. He went off to try it on, to return looking a real gent. The outfitter added a bow tie but we decided to dispense with the cummerbund. 'I hope no one I know sees me dressed like this,' said Eddie, laughing.

'You look very smart,' I said. We also bought two lovely white shirts, one with a frill down the front, and two beautiful jackets that he could wear with different trousers for semi-formal nights. They remained in the wardrobe, holding their memories.

I tried going to bed but sleep was impossible. I watched TV until the early hours, drank tea, tried to read, but most of all I pondered and worried, worried and pondered. What was I going to do?

I wish I could say that by breakfast I had decided. I'd had around two hours' troubled sleep and woke feeling awful, my mind as usual in turmoil. I felt as if I were drowning in a thick morass, lost and so alone. What should I do? Eventually, as I climbed into the car, I decided to cling onto one thought which had to be the most important: what was the best for Eddie?

I don't remember the drive, I don't remember if it was dry or raining, I don't remember if I saw anyone I knew on the road. I must have gone on automatic, my mind far away. I suppose I mainly thought about Eddie, the boy he was, the man he became. The village school he attended during the war years, the stories he'd told me, like the day when he and his Aunty Mary went to a farm outside the village after dark to collect part of a black-market pig. They brought it back in a wheelbarrow. 'We had an awful job pushing it back home,' he said. 'It was that heavy, and we were feared of being caught.'

He told me about gas-mask drills at school. 'When teacher said, we all had to pull them out and put them on. Nasty, uncomfortable things they were. Then we'd sit there, looking like a load of pigs.' There were soldiers stationed in the village and Eddie collected badges from them; he said how exciting it was seeing Bren-guns parked around the village and tanks practising up on the Scar.

He used to laugh when he told me how he nearly blew

up The Mill. 'I used to find shells up the fields and bring them home. I had a few stores around the farm and a secret one in the house. Somehow the police found out and the constable turned up one day. I had to show him where they were. Seems some of them were still live and they soon had them away. Mam and Dad were fair put-out.' At this point in the story he would give a wicked grin. 'But they didn't find them all. I had some well-tucked away outside.' I expect they're still lying in some forgotten hidey-hole.

After leaving school at fourteen, Eddie started work, splitting his time between the farm and a joinery apprenticeship. It must have been a hard life for a young boy: up early, walking all over the area carrying his tools to the job, walking home after a full day's work, then starting with his farm chores. But this gave him a strong work ethic, which stayed with him all his life, and I never heard him complain.

He did find time for a bit of fun, mainly through the Young Farmers Club. He went to socials and became involved in plays and concerts. He enjoyed music and dancing, although he never mastered either art. He went to church and chapel, though never on a regular basis as he got older. He always prided himself on introducing the first Friesian dairy cow to the area, much to the disapproval of the older farmers, and he once made the local papers when it became known he liked to milk the cows to music. 'It relaxes them and helps them to "let their milk down",' he told the reporter. He also went on day trips to Blackpool which gave him a lifelong love of the place. I suppose it was such a change from the quietness of the farm and village, all the glitz and noise. He enjoyed the funfair and the hair-raising rides.

Thinking about it, I suppose Eddie's life had been hard but full. He'd had a stable home and family and spent his years doing a job he enjoyed. He understood farm animals, working with the old plough-horse as a boy, keeping pigs and cows as he grew older. He'd these big, strong farmer's hands, the top of one finger lopped off by the milking machine years before. He had a saying which he often quoted: 'The land is faithful'. He'd kept faith with that land and his home all his life.

I'd made my decision by the time I turned into the Silverdown car park. I went through the signing-in ritual and was greeted as always by smiles from the staff. Eddie was dozing in an armchair, so I went straight to the office to speak to Carol. Perhaps it was because I'd made up my mind that I managed to keep calm for once. 'I've decided that Eddie should stay,' I said.

She took my hand. 'You've made the right decision. You know we'll look after him and you can see him whenever you want to.'

We spent the next half hour on practicalities. 'Do you want him to have the same room?' Carol asked. 'One of the upgraded ones is available upstairs but it's much smaller and we tend to have the severely ill patients up there.'

'No, I think we'll leave him in the room he's used to.'

'That's fine. Now he's stopping, bring anything you think he'd like having around. Objects that hold memories, photographs, pictures. You might like to purchase some pieces of new furniture. That's fine. Oh, and he'll need the remainder of his clothes.'

Talking of clothing brought back an incident that had distressed me a few days before. I'd turned up to see Eddie and found him dressed in pants, shirt and jumper that weren't his. They were old and of poor quality and I'd complained to the staff. I'd discovered that all the patients' laundry went off together for cleaning then was sorted in the linen cupboard. All the clothing was marked with the patients' names, and they were then put in the correct pile ready to be taken back to their rooms. I was told that, because Eddie's clothes were unmarked, they'd ended up in the spare-clothes section. I'd been shown the cupboard and fished around, finding his clean laundry. 'I'll have them all marked before I bring them in,' I said. Then we discussed finance.

There were papers to take home, read and sign; there were now a lot of extra problems to get my head around but they could wait until tomorrow. There are only so many dilemmas one can face at any one time.

I'd used up our two weeks, fourteen days, 336 hours. I'd cried, worried myself sick, deliberated and agonised, leading to this crucial moment in our lives. This is where the journey had led and I now had to face the reality: after seventy-nine years, Eddie would never live in his home again.

PROLOGUE TO PART 2

In the scale of grief, ours is a small tale. Every day millions of people encounter terrible pain and suffering, both personal and involving loved ones, young and old. There are countless untold stories, all deserving a hearing. Why would anyone be interested in ours? What happened to Eddie and me is not unique; it's happening on a similar scale to many others and, with an ageing population, more and more cases of all forms of dementia will occur.

Perhaps that's the real reason for writing this. We were not unique. Thousands of patients and their carers are struggling to cope with the fickle finger of dementia. Lives are being disrupted and futures destroyed. Some are overcome with the illness much younger; others are afflicted for a number of years. The decline can be gradual but in others, like Eddie, rapid. Perhaps all those people need to know they are not alone, they are not unique, that the way they feel and the problems they encounter are shared by thousands.

The government and the health services are at last waking up to this problem, which can only grow worse. Modern medicine and operating techniques, added to other health factors, are keeping people alive longer, giving longevity, but that also allows time for dementia to develop. Yet there are still few purpose-built homes for dementia patients who, on many occasions, have to be placed in an ordinary care home or in a small unit attached to a care home.

This is where I was extremely lucky, as Silverdown had

been built specifically for the care of dementia patients and was structured to help and provide nursing for them through to the end of life. The staff, a combination of trained nurses and qualified carers, understood how to approach dementia and deal with the many physical and mental problems it involved. So, even though it felt like my heart was being torn, I knew Eddie would be well looked after.

PART TWO

SILVERDOWN

CHAPTER 8

CHANGE

The following morning, I went into town to purchase some printed name tapes to attach to Eddie's clothes. I could do without the added upset of seeing him dressed in someone else's cast-offs. He was not a waif and stray and there was no way he was ever going to look like one.

Thinking back, it's strange that how he was dressed became so important. Maybe it was because, apart from when he was working around the farm, he'd always been very particular about his appearance. It was now my responsibility to ensure this continued. I was no longer there to dress him but I was determined that those who were would dress him correctly. Perhaps this worry was a way of making Eddie's permanent departure from his home more manageable. Think about the clothes; the rest will follow.

Once home, I sorted through the wardrobe and removed all his vests, shirts, trousers, jumpers, pyjamas and socks. I'd forgotten how many clothes he had but thankfully I'd bought a couple of hundred name tapes. I loaded and packed the car and drove down to my friend Pat. I sorted the clothes and cut the tapes; she ironed while we chatted and, of course, I wept. Her husband had died some time before. 'At least you can still go and see him,' she said.

Perhaps it seems trivial at such a time to dwell on ironing name tapes but it was another problem that needed sorting.

There was no point in taking his clothes to Silverdown before they were marked; since he needed regular changes, it was an urgent problem that needed resolving.

Getting my head around new worries took some doing. I was so emotionally charged, so tired, so wrung-out, that I really didn't want to do anything but visit Eddie. But there was only me left, and I had to face reality.

I telephoned Eden Alarms to come and remove the ones they'd fitted and I went into the bank to make an appointment to see someone about our finances. I also had to face the guilt-ridden prospect of telling people that Eddie would be staying in Silverdown.

To my face, everyone was very sympathetic and understanding; what they said behind my back I'll never know. I do know that Eddie's sister and my close friends were fully supportive; knowing how hard the last twelve months had been, they realised I'd had no choice. I hope that people who didn't know me so well felt the same, but in the past I'd been unjustly judgemental and I couldn't blame people if they felt the same.

What else to take to brighten his room and harness memories? I chose a beautifully embroidered tablecloth that we'd bought in Sorrento on one of our cruises. I also took a large framed photograph. Eddie loved this picture that I'd found tucked away in the house shortly after we were married. 'I didn't know we still had that,' he'd said laughing. It was a two-foot square, black-and-white picture taken in the middle of a road, showing a baby in a pram.

'Where was it?' I'd asked.

'On the road just outside the village.'

'Is it you?'

'On no, that's our Bobby. He'd be about one. Mam would have been out for a walk.'

'You couldn't leave a pram in that road these days, it would get flattened,' I'd said. 'It's lovely, we must put it up somewhere.' After that it had hung on the staircase wall for many years. This picture, along with one of The Old Mill when the wheel was still there, went with him to Silverdown. I also took a wedding photo: small trimmings, small pieces of Eddie's old life transported into his new.

From now on I lived in two worlds, both strange, both unreal. When Eddie had been admitted into Silverdown for the two weeks' respite, I'd been marking time, mainly preparing for his return, never really facing the possibility that his departure would be permanent. Now all that changed and, for the first time in my life, I was alone.

I soon realised that being alone and being lonely were two different things. As an only child, I'd had to make my own entertainment; I grew up enjoying my own company, I never craved other children. I liked having friends around but when they weren't there I didn't miss them. I always had many hobbies and interests and these continued as I grew up. Now I had to face the truth that I would be living alone for the rest of my life. This was no temporary arrangement, this was not someone being absent for a while, this was my life from now on, just me and the cats.

I suppose it was the physical lack of another human being that hit me most. No other permanent presence in the house, no sounds of movement, no other voice except the radio or television. When I went out, the house was left empty and alone; no one would enter until I returned. When I did return, the house would be as I'd left it, dark and quiet apart from the cats expecting food and care. I've always loved animals, especially cats, and now they became more important than ever. They didn't speak but they moved and breathed, gave some semblance of life to my home. They were no substitute to my jovial husband; they couldn't put the kettle on, ask me how my day had gone, stoke the Rayburn or share a joke, but they demanded my attention and to a small degree helped to minimise the emptiness.

Now I could go to bed when I chose, enter a room where only I would sleep. Never again would I wake to the sound of another's breath, hear a toilet flush in the night, or say 'Good morning' to anyone. When dawn came, unless I had some pressing engagement, I could rise when I wanted. I had no one but myself to please, no one else to consider.

I was still physically exhausted but also primed to wake many times during the night. I was to find this habit difficult to break and it was many months before I could sleep for more than two hours at a time. The worst time was that morning awakening. It was winter, so dawn came slowly as consciousness crept over me. The emptiness felt like an ache; something was always missing. It was Eddie.

Thirty-five years is a long time to wake up next to someone and, for others in a similar situation, it may have been many more years. Never underestimate the devastation of that separation, the feeling of loss. The quietness as you slip out of bed, pull the curtains, shower, dress and walk alone down into the morning silence of the house. A solitary breakfast, no one to share the latest news, no one to tell what your plans are for the day.

Modern technology helped me to cope. I'd bought a portable DVD player some months before. Now I kept it at my bedside and took to watching something on it each morning. Serials and films, twenty minutes at a time and continued the next morning, became my routine. This had a twofold benefit: whatever I was watching filled both my mind and the silence.

I also functioned in two separate existences. At home I

shopped, saw friends and went here and there. Every day someone asked about Eddie, so I talked about him regularly. Outwardly I must have appeared unchanged and to be coping well with a sad situation. I would then climb in the car and drive to Silverdown.

I went most days. From the minute I drove into the car park, I left one world behind and entered another. In through the door, sign in, sanitise my hands, speak into the intercom, then the door would be opened. I usually arrived around 10 to 10.30, when Eddie was sitting in the main day room. Sometimes we shared a couch, other times I pulled up a chair beside him. Tea and biscuits would arrive; some days he was chatty, other days quiet and sleepy.

I'd been given a key for his room, so I'd go and check his clothes were in order and that he didn't need anything replacing. Gradually I added more items from home to his room: more pictures, a CD player with his favourite music. He loved Foster and Allen, The Five-Penny Piece and Jim Reeves. The staff said they put the music on for him if he wanted to go to bed during the day or in an evening.

Sometimes when I went, even though the home was very warm and he was wearing a thick jumper, he appeared cold. The staff provided extra blankets but I bought him some fleecy ones of his own. He would snuggle into them, often pulling one over his head and refusing to come out. On these occasions I'd peep under the blanket. 'Hello Eddie, are you going to come out and talk to me?' Sometimes he did; other times he stayed beneath his blanket the whole time I was there, either hiding or asleep.

These were the worst days. When I couldn't talk to him, I would sit and think and end up fighting my tears. As these days became more frequent, I took to writing short poems, just anything that came into my mind in those surreal moments.

> Beneath a blanket, sunk into a jacket blue
> You doze, chin on chest,
> You rest within your made-up world,
> I in mine. But it is fine by me.
> You do not know I wade in waves
> Of sadness every day, as you
> Slowly, oh so slowly, slip away.

Around this time I had a visit from someone from the Council to discuss our finances. I'd received a letter from her prior to the visit. I had to have documented proof of what money or investments we held. I'd spent the afternoon searching through the filing cabinet. My papers were in a mess; for months I'd had neither the time nor inclination to keep files up to date. I had piles of paper everywhere and was getting more and more frustrated and upset. How could I be expected to deal with money when I was spinning in a sea of confusion and sorrow?

We weren't wealthy but we were comfortable; hopefully, with careful budgeting, we'd reckoned we'd have enough savings to see us through. This would allow for general expenses, car replacement, necessary house maintenance and, until Eddie became ill, regular holidays. Our income was small: we had our pensions, Eddie had a tiny private pension, and we had the yearly rent from our thirty-five acres of land. We owned the house and farm but still had regular outgoings like everyone else – electricity, water, heating, Council Tax and living costs.

The woman from the Council was efficient, business-like and did not indulge in small talk. She came across as cold and unsympathetic but that could have been part of her job or my general state of mind. She shuffled through my documents, making notes, asking pertinent questions.

From Eddie's admission to Silverdown, we'd been self-financing: the cost was just over £2,000 per month. It seems an astronomical amount to have to find but other homes in the area, which were not dedicated dementia homes and only had a small unit attached, were far more expensive, some coming in at over £800 a week. The purpose of the visit was to assess how long I could manage to pay for Eddie and when the Council might step in.

I've thought about this conundrum many times, both then and in the intervening years. Eddie had worked hard all his life, up at 6am, rarely finishing until 8pm. For the twenty-eight years we'd had the milk round, we'd worked side by side: a 5am start, struggling out in all weathers with the milk. When Eddie got home he went straight to milk the cows and during the day I would wash bottles in the icy-cold dairy. We usually bottled together unless he was busy with a cow calving or during hay time. For over twenty years we'd never managed a holiday. I'd seen Eddie go out to milk the cows, dragging himself along with flu. It didn't matter if it was his birthday or Christmas Day, the cows still had to be milked twice daily.

When we retired, we expected to have a good number of years to relax and enjoy ourselves. We'd had barely three, but thank God we'd crammed all those holidays into that short time and also spent a sizeable chunk of our holiday fund. Now our hard-earned savings would be gradually drained away by Eddie's care – yet, if we'd not owned our own farm but lived in rented property, if we'd not worked hard and saved, if we'd lived hand to mouth, Eddie's care would have been paid for by the Council.

It all felt so damned unfair! At the time I felt deeply

aggrieved, thinking we were being punished for daring to work hard and save. Apart from our pensions, we never received a penny from the state until Eddie was awarded attendance allowance. We'd paid taxes all our lives and never owed anyone anything. On the other hand, I suppose there's a case for saying: well if you can afford it you should pay. Why should the state provide? Yes, it's a conundrum.

The Council lady added everything up and declared that, as our finances stood at the moment, Eddie would have to pay his way for some months to come. She said I must go to the bank and split our savings down the middle: half was mine and could not be touched; Eddie's half must be reduced to a certain level before he could be reassessed for help. The house was safe because I was living in it but the land was a different matter: this would be counted as an asset. When Eddie's share of the money had been reduced then the land would be taken into account. Most likely, she said, it would have to be sold. I would keep half of the proceeds and the other half would have to be used to pay for Silverdown. By the time she left, I was trembling with worry and feeling physically sick.

I'd expected the conclusion she'd reached about our monetary savings and I knew the house was safe, but the land – that came as a blow. This land, this precious, fruitful land, which had been passed down to Eddie through the generations; this land which he loved, worked and trod countless miles across during his lifetime, would have to be sold.

In my mind I saw him trundling along on his tractor, bent over a wall, putting in fences, cutting nettles, spreading fertiliser or farmyard manure, hay-timing, or the daily spring and summer walk up and down the fields to bring in the cows. I pictured him booting dandelions, eating sandwiches propped against a wall with such a look of peace and happiness, or leaning against a cart watching the passing clouds. Up there in the top fields he saw the seasons change year by year, he listened to the birds, absorbed the tranquillity of the countryside.

Over the years I'd grown to love this land as much as he did. Even though it was now rented out, it was still ours and I still felt his presence upon it. The thought that it must be sold, that someone else would claim ownership to Eddie's land, was appalling. Plus, the regular yearly rent was important for our finances and paid a good chunk of our essential bills.

It wasn't an immediate problem but would loom larger as the months wore away. At that moment, I think I felt like Scarlett O'Hara in Gone with the Wind, clutching a handful of soil with a grim determination to do everything in my power to hold onto that land, to fight. I decided to wait until the New Year then see a solicitor and seek legal advice.

I did go to the bank and organise the separating of our funds but it wasn't easy. I was not in the right frame of mind to work out what needed doing but the bank was very kind and helpful, and somehow I got through it.

There was another problem that I had to grasp. I'd been advised to sort out the power of attorney. The papers were still at home, filled in but unsigned. Now the Silverdown management said that if it was still possible, it should be done. It was agreed that I should arrange a meeting at the home with Eddie's GP, Carol and myself, to see if Eddie could not only sign the forms but if he would understand what he was signing.

It was around two weeks before Christmas. We went into a side room. Eddie was having a day when he was quite alert. I think I knew from the moment we sat down that it was going to be a waste of time.

He'd known our doctor for a number of years but now he hadn't a clue who she was. She was very patient and tried to explain what was going on. Eddie just smiled and nodded, oblivious to her explanations. She asked him a few simple questions.

'Do you know where you are?'

'That's an easy one,' he said with a laugh. 'I'm at The Mill, of course.'

'Do you know who this is, Eddie?' she asked, pointing to Carol.

'Not a clue but she's a nice lass.'

'How about this lady, Eddie?' she asked, indicating me.

'Why, that's a daft question! That's our Ruby.' We gave up after that.

'I'm sorry, Jackie,' she said. 'He has to know what the forms are about. Sadly, he doesn't even know you today and I doubt he could hold a pen.'

So that was that; hopefully the power of attorney would not be needed. All our finances had been in joint names and the home had already recognised that it was me to whom they referred about anything to do with Eddie's care. This became important soon afterwards.

I received an urgent phone call from the home a few days later to say that Eddie had been having chest pains and they'd sent for the doctor, who wanted him transferred to Carlisle Hospital. I jumped in the car and headed off immediately. I'd invested a few weeks before in winter tyres so I'd be able to reach Eddie no matter what the weather conditions. It was a journey that took just over twenty minutes but the doctor had left when I arrived and the ambulance was waiting.

'He's worried Eddie's had a heart attack,' said the nurse on duty. 'He's actually much better now. We've given him his angina spray and the pain has almost gone, but the doctor was insistent. The paramedics are with him, getting him ready.'

I went through to Eddie's room, where he was lying on the bed, wired up to a heart monitor.

'This is his wife,' said the nurse.

'Don't worry, we're just checking him over then we'll be off. He seems stable but we'll keep the monitor on,' one of the paramedics said.

I went to Eddie and took his hand, trying to keep calm. His usual red-rubbed cheeks were a little pale.

'Don't know what all the fuss is about,' he said. 'I was just off for the cows when all these folk piled in.'

'We're going to take you up to the hospital for a bit of a check-up, Eddie,' said one of the paramedics. 'Do you want to come in the ambulance with him?' they asked me.

I had to think quickly. If I went in the ambulance and they admitted him, how would I get home? If I followed in my car I wouldn't be stranded or have to bother anyone else, but would he become distressed if I wasn't with him? I decided to trust the professionalism of the ambulance men. 'No, I'll drive.'

'Fine. We'll be away in a few minutes. He'll be going to A&E.'

Helped by the nurse, I packed Eddie an overnight bag in case it was needed. A short while later, well wrapped up in blankets against the cold, he was placed in the back of the ambulance. Seconds later they were off with blue flasher going, me in tow.

There was no way I could match their speed but traffic was fairly light with it being that time of the year. I lost them on the motorway but must have reached the hospital only a little while after them.

There is a large car-parking area outside the main hospital buildings with room for a few hundred cars but, though I drove up and down, it was crammed to capacity, with cars even drawn up on the grass verges. I realised it was visiting time, plus the regular clinics would be working; it felt like half of Carlisle had packed into the hospital. In rising panic, I headed for the other large car park at the furthest end of the hospital and, after much searching, found one space in a remote corner. I fumbled for change and raced off to find a parking meter, then back to put the ticket in the window. From where I was parked it was a ten-minute walk to A&E but I did it in five, running, clutching the overnight bag.

I've never been much of a runner, even when I was younger, but rising worry drove me on. Would the ambulance men be able to stay with Eddie, or would he be left alone? Would he become frightened, not understanding where he was? Would the staff know he'd got dementia and was deaf? I had no idea what the doctor had put in the letter which he'd sent with him. What if he had another heart attack before I reached him?

I was shaking, and gasping for breath when I eventually reached the main entrance. With difficulty, I found my way to A&E. After hanging around in their waiting room, I was eventually allowed into the department and shown to Eddie's cubicle.

To my relief, one of the paramedics was still with him and Eddie looked none the worse for his journey. He was attached to a heart monitor, which was bleeping steadily. 'I'll be off now the wife's here, Eddie,' the paramedic said, shaking his hand.

'What time's the train due?' Eddie asked, as I pulled a chair up to his side. 'There's such a lot of people for the train today,' he continued, pointing to the small gap in the curtains. As always, A&E was busy and I could see doctors, nurses, patients and relatives moving back and forth. 'Did you did get the tickets?' We'd been here before; I wondered what station we were on this time, and where we were off to.

'Yes,' I assured him. 'Have you got any chest pain now?'

He looked at me puzzled. 'Chest pain? Oh, I'm fine. Don't know what all these wires and things are about. Take the damn things off, Jackie.' He reached to detach himself. I sprang up, gently taking his hands away and pulling the blanket over his chest.

'It's just for a short while. They'll move them soon. You lie quiet and relax.'

'This bed's uncomfortable but it's you I'm worried about. If you don't get a move on, you'll miss the match.'

I was having trouble keeping up but I was expecting a long wait, so I suspended logic and entered into his world. 'Aren't you coming with me?'

'I've a cow down and the vet's due, but I want you to go. There's a chance Carlisle might win today, and you wouldn't want to miss it.' I wasn't sure when I'd become a Carlisle United supporter; to my knowledge, the last time I'd set foot in a stadium was in my teens when I went to Old Trafford to watch Manchester United. 'Les is going as well,' he added. That cleared things up a bit: his old friend Les would never miss a Carlisle match, but sadly he'd been dead a few years.

We spent the next twenty minutes discussing football, the price of train tickets, and how busy Crewe station was today. I'm not sure when we decamped from Carlisle to Crewe.

Eventually a doctor came in to clarify why Eddie was there and give him an examination. He unwisely addressed his questions to Eddie. 'Mr Huck? I believe you've been having some chest pains.'

Eddie, looking at me: 'Can't hear a word he's saying.'

Me to the doctor: 'He's rather deaf. I've put his hearing aids in and he should hear you if you speak quite loud and distinctly.'

The question was repeated and this time Eddie heard, but hearing and understanding were different matters. 'We're just waiting for the train. We're off to Edinburgh. Are you going as well?' I tried to work out when Edinburgh had come into the equation.

The doctor tried again. 'You've had some pains in your chest. How do you feel now?'

Eddie was having another go at dislodging the heart-monitor wires. 'I can't stay here and I don't know what these bits and pieces are about. I've a cow to drench.' He turned to me. 'Have you got the horn ready? You'll have to hold her tail up while I pour the liquid in.'

At this point the monitor started making strange noises, the doctor leapt to the wires and I grabbed Eddie's hands. The alarm created a small stampede of doctors and nurses who arrived at the cubicle to be assured all was well. Calm was restored.

The doctor now carefully studied the letter which had accompanied Eddie and watched the heart monitor, which was again dutifully beeping in a regular, controlled manner. With difficulty he took Eddie's pulse and blood pressure, then he had one final try. 'You've had chest pains, Mr Huck, and you're in hospital.'

Eddie gave him a wide smile then one of those looks reserved for an idiot. 'Don't be so daft. Me and the wife are going to Blackpool and if we don't get a move on we'll miss our train.'

'I'll go and have a word with my boss,' said the doctor, making a hasty get-away. Eddie was also ready for a 'hasty get-away' as he tried to throw a leg off the trolley. I managed to settle him again before the heart monitor kicked off. It was so tragically funny.

A while passed; we'd been there approaching two hours. A nurse came in, checked the monitor and removed the wires. 'If you need someone urgently, just press that button,' she said.

Eventually the senior doctor turned up and introduced himself. He was a middle-aged man with a kind face and an air of knowledgeable professionalism. I can't remember if he was a cardiac specialist or the senior casualty officer. 'How you doing, old chap?' he asked. 'I hear you've not been too well.' He spoke clearly, taking Eddie's hand and checking his pulse while he spoke.

'I'm grand,' said Eddie. 'I just want to be away home.'

'Fine, I'll be back in a few minutes.' He turned to me. 'Shall we go and have a chat?'

I followed him out of the cubicle, down a corridor, and into a deserted office. He flicked on the light and indicated a chair. He settled himself across from me. 'Your husband's seventy-nine, Mrs Huck.' I nodded. 'And he's suffering from advanced vascular dementia. You do know the outcome?'

I swallowed. I must keep calm. 'Yes. It's galloped on this last twelve months.'

'That's why he's in Silverdown?' the consultant asked.

'Yes, we just couldn't manage at home any longer.'

'He does know who you are?'

'Today, but not always.'

'I'm going to lay my cards on the table,' he said. 'I could admit him and do various tests to check if he's had a heart attack. I don't think he has – I think it was a bad angina attack and he's fine now. If I admit him, he'll be in for a day or two, but—' he paused '—is there any point? You know his condition will continue to deteriorate. It's just a matter of time. He's no idea what is going on. Is any useful purpose being served by admitting him?'

That was quite a statement to take in and I could feel emotion welling up. We were sitting with 'the elephant in the room' again: a different doctor, a different setting, the same elephant. Eddie was going to die; was there any point doing investigations and perhaps prescribing extra medication to prolong his life?

He wasn't going to get better, he wasn't going to improve. Oh, there would be some good days, but this was a boulder rolling down a hill and nothing could stop it reaching the bottom. He was already incontinent and this would become double incontinence. He would soon become immobile, need virtually everything done for him and, if he lived long enough, he would be unable to speak or even swallow. Did I really want to prolong his life for that? God! Life is cruel!

'I could just send him back to his care home,' the doctor said. 'Is that what you would prefer?'

I struggled to speak but managed. 'Yes, that's what I want.'

'Also,' he continued, 'should he have a similar attack, or any other medical emergency, would you like me to write to his doctor and have the letter put in his notes, that he's not to be sent to hospital again?'

I felt I'd come a full circle: we were back with the aneurism, life or death, my decision, but this time it was easier to make. I loved Eddie too much to have people struggle to keep him alive for him to face the last terrible symptoms of dementia. 'Yes please,' I said.

So that was the end of it. Eddie was officially discharged back to Silverdown. The department was heaving, and I was told it would be a two-hour wait for an ambulance. 'Is it okay to take him back in my car?' I asked. Perhaps it was a gamble but I'd come to the conclusion that every day now would be a gamble so there was nothing to lose. I was told that would be fine. I left Eddie in the care of a nurse while I rushed off to collect the car and bring it round to the A&E entrance.

He was loaded into a wheelchair and the nurse helped him into the car. With Eddie happily laughing that we were at last going to see their Ruby, we drove away.

It was an uneventful journey. As we chatted, Eddie cracked on about cows and things he remembered when he was a boy; those memories were still very clear. He talked about his mum and dad as if they were still waiting at home and, of course, about Bobby, who we'd just left after seeing him in Melton Mowbray.

'He looked well,' said Eddie, as we came off the motorway. 'We must go again soon. He's that busy, he doesn't get up to the The Mill often these days.' I drove around the roundabout, onto the A6. Silverdown was only a few minutes away. Eddie continued to chatter; he was really bright and completely contented in this world he'd created.

A short way down the A6 I had to turn right to Silverdown. If I carried straight on, we'd be home in twenty minutes. Oh how I wanted to drive straight on. I pictured me taking him home up that well-known track. I still had the wheelchair; I could get him out of the car and settle him in front of the telly. I'd soon have the house warm and tea on the boil. I could cuddle and care for him and be always there for him through to the end. This had been a blip; there was no need for him to be in a home. He was my special, precious man; how could I take him back to Silverdown?

Up to the second I reached the turn-off, I didn't know which way I would go. Ahead? Right? Ahead? I felt as if I were sitting in a bath of icy water as my hands gripped the steering wheel until they hurt. As we neared the turning, reality started to establish itself and I went over the reasons Eddie was in Silverdown. With a sigh, I turned right and took him back.

Christmas 2011 loomed and, as with the previous Christmas, I remember little about it. I sent out the usual cards and put up the Christmas tree. I must have bought and wrapped some presents but most of the preparations are a blur. Anything I did get around to was fitted around a daily visit to Eddie.

The staff worked hard to make Silverdown as jolly as possible for the festive season, putting up decorations and dressing a large tree. This was carefully placed so none of the residents would fall over it but that did not protect it from attack. Some of 'the wanderers' felt it was their task in life to either rearrange the ornaments or demolish the thing entirely. Quite often during one of my visits the tree would be in trouble and a carer would have to dash to its rescue. All the tree baubles were plastic so took no harm, but they regularly were seen rolling along, being kicked by a slippered foot. Also, a few patients took to slamming their wheelchairs into the tree, then a quick rugby tackle was needed to prevent its destruction. The carers just laughed and carried on with their work.

Eddie was oblivious to Christmas. If he noticed the tree at all, he believed it to be one of the trees he passed as he walked up to get the cows. On the odd occasion he noticed a decoration, he asked whose birthday it was.

The 11th December was the Silverdown Christmas party for patients and relatives. For me, as on many other occasions, it was a strange experience and one I wrote about that evening when I returned home.

'What can I write about a Christmas party in a care

home for dementia patients, when the majority have no conception of where they are or what's going on and it could be Christmas or the middle of summer?

Eddie smiles as I arrive, so that's a good start. Today he knows who I am. I've come to recognise most of the patients by now and, like Eddie, accept them as they are. A lot more relatives here than most days. A few I know a little, most are strangers, each have been on their own sad journey. Love keeps them going, love binds us together,

Eddie is sure we're at a hotel in Morecambe, the big white one on the front, but it's too cold for a walk on the sands this morning, he says. He's tired, he's spent all day cooking and cleaning, so many pots and pans to wash, he's worn out.

Maisie wanders past. I don't think she has any visiting relatives today. She spends her days wandering, her green cardigan buttoned up wrong as always, an anguished expression creasing her worn face. One hand clutching the crotch of her brown pants, she heads for a window and spends time tracing the frame. This now is Maisie's life, a continuous wander to nowhere.

Eddie is obsessing about his shoes as the afternoon entertainer begins to sing. I ask one of the carers about them (he only has his socks on). She says his feet were swollen this morning and nothing would fit. I make a mental note to buy a fresh pair of slippers larger than his usual size ten. The singing booms out 'I'm a Believer' by The Monkees. Eddie slips into a doze.

He wakes after half an hour, the singer is still in full voice. I suppose some are listening. Eddie holds my hand, stroking and caressing the soft flesh – no, I must not cry! God damn it, I must not cry! His socks have become his shoes and they need fastening. I assure him they're okay. No, he says, the socks have got holes in. I laugh. 'I wouldn't let you walk round in holey socks.'

We've left Morecambe, now we're up at a farm just outside the village. Two farming neighbours are holding a party for relatives and friends and Eddie is really set up that we've been invited. He laughs, asking them how the sheep and cows are doing, and what about the market prices.

Sam comes to sit in front of us with his wife and two other relatives. He's fairly quiet today, I've seen him starting fights with other patients and he regularly stands over us swearing. One of the first times I visited, his wife fled in tears after he swore repeatedly at her. She remembers the man he was. Love brings her back, love helps her to hold on – I know.

It's time to draw the raffle. Every patient has been given a free raffle ticket, so there's a prize for all. The staff must have been collecting the gifts together for a long time. We're now in the social club at the next village and the new vicar is drawing the raffle. I'm amazed as our ticket comes out second. I always say the booby prize is reserved for me. I choose a tin of Quality Street, one of Eddie's favourites.

We're back at the farming party. 'I didn't realise what a big family they have,' says Eddie, 'and all squashed into this small farmhouse. Mind you, Alice is a great cook, used to win lots of prizes.' He turns to a lady seated nearby. 'Are you her daughter?' She knows the form and plays along, says she's just a friend.

It's time for the buffet. I get two plates with sandwiches and sausage rolls. Eddie's not hungry but tucks in and eats the lot. We have mince pies and cheesecake for dessert. 'I told you Alice was a good cook,' Eddie says as he clears up the crumbs.

The music is over. Some relatives linger, others slip away. I put Eddie's Quality Street in his room and check if he's any clothes in the laundry store. I've given Sam's wife my card and told her to phone me if she needs to talk; we all need support.

'I enjoyed Bobby's birthday party,' Eddie says. 'Best one he's had.' He is growing tired, his eyes closing. It's time to leave, I kiss him. He yawns and smiles.

I head for the door. 'I'll be back tomorrow.'

***

It was arranged that I would go on Christmas Day and Eddie and I would have the special Christmas dinner with all the trimmings. I went to church that morning, singing in the choir. There were a number of people in the congregation, the tree was lit with lights, and there was such a feeling of warmth and family togetherness. I only managed one verse of 'Silent Night' before the tears threatened. I was hidden behind a pillar in the choir stalls so no one in church knew, but Angela's comforting hand strayed onto mine.

I arrived at Silverdown in good time, clutching a large tin of chocolate biscuits for the staff. It was difficult to give them a present they could all share but I expect they received many gifts and perhaps were able to each choose what they fancied. I took Eddie a new woolly blanket and a book with horse pictures, which triggered memories of Johnny the plough horse, and Buttons, who was the family pony when Eddie was small.

At first he seemed quite bright and we had a little chat and looked at the pictures. He was wobbly on his legs, so two of the carers supported him as he walked to the decorated Christmas table. I sat next to him and the soup was served. I had mine but Eddie only took a little and appeared to be getting quiet and distant. The main course arrived, with the turkey, stuffing, apple sauce, potatoes and all the vegetables.

Not a large plate for Eddie; they knew he enjoyed smaller meals.

He took a few bites, played around with the potato, then suddenly slumped forwards in his chair, head down on his chest, hands slipping limply away. I steadied him and summoned one of the carers who went for the nurse. She arrived and took his pulse, a concerned look on her face. Between us we held him, me calling his name, 'Eddie, Eddie.'

He started to regain consciousness after about three minutes. He was still rather floppy, but at least his eyes were open and he was yawning.

'He's had a few of these attacks,' said the nurse. I did know; it was similar to the attack on the day of his arrival. 'Do you want any more dinner, Eddie?' she asked. He shook his head. 'Don't worry,' she said to me. 'We'll keep it in the kitchen with some pudding and custard, and warm it up later when he feel like eating. I think we'd better put him to bed for the time being.'

He was transferred into a wheelchair and taken to his room. 'We'll just take his jumper off but leave the rest. He'll most likely want to be up and about again later. Do you want to sit with him? We can bring your dinner through to the table?' So Eddie was tucked up in bed, and the nurse checked his blood pressure which was a bit low. 'I'll take it again in a while.'

A new hot Christmas dinner was laid for me, with pudding to follow. I sat in the silent room eating the saddest, strangest Christmas dinner I'd ever had. I wasn't really hungry but felt I had to eat the meal since they'd laid it out so nicely for me, and there was little else I could do.

The afternoon wore on and Eddie slept. The nurse came back every half hour to check his pulse and blood pressure. 'They're both normal,' she assured me. 'I don't think we need to phone the doctor. He should be fine when he wakes up.'

Mid-afternoon he stirred and sat up in bed. 'Do you want a cup of tea?' the nurse asked. 'Or anything to eat?'

'Just a cup of tea,' he said. We shared a drink, then he settled back down and was soon asleep.

For a while I sat by his bedside, stroking his thinning grey hair. He looked so peaceful yet frail, but his breathing was normal and I agreed he would be fine when he woke later. I knew I would break down if I stayed any longer. It was the accumulation of all the heartache that the year had brought and seeing him like this, added to the general emotion that accompanies Christmas.

I left just before dark, slipping away quietly.

CHAPTER 9

2012

I have never managed to keep a diary. I would be bought one for Christmas most years and make dutiful entries for the first week or two, only for this to taper away until eventually page after page remained blank as if my life had stopped. How I wish I could look back to various years, especially my teens and twenties, and recall in detail what I did day by day. It is strange, then, that the only year I kept an accurate and regular diary was 2012. I have it still but will burn it when I've finished recording this journey.

I copy now the first entry, for January 1st.

It's the sort of year that I feel I must keep a diary. Nationally, it's the year of the London Olympics and the Queen's Diamond Jubilee; personally it's the year of the unknown. How rapidly will Eddie's dementia grow worse? Will he go completely off his legs? Will he still be alive on January 1st 2013 and, if so, what state will he be in?

I'm afraid of this year. Last year was an increasing nightmare, building to the terrible decision to leave him in Silverdown. Now I float in this limbo world, heading for the ultimate sad ending. There is no hope in this scenario. Somehow I will have to keep going and remain strong.

I awoke at 6am this morning. I'm not going to see

Eddie today but went off to church. Everyone is kind, wishing me Happy New Year, but the reply stuck in my throat and I slipped away quickly after the service as I couldn't trust myself to talk.

1.30, I went across to the bungalow to have a meal with my neighbours, Charlie, David and Nick. They have been so caring, coming across to help with Eddie before he was admitted to Silverdown and supporting me with their words and friendship since. I had a lovely afternoon with them, managing to relax in their company and even feel a little happy for a short while.

Curled up with TV and the cats in the evening. So the year begins.

***

When I came to write about 'The Journey', I knew the early months would be difficult to recall because all I had were an unconnected bunch of notes, the calendar and my scattered memories. I thought 2012 would be so much easier as I had the diary to follow, but that's not true. As I put my mind back to that year, I find the diary repetitive, the days merging and following a similar pattern. Others in a comparable situation will feel the same: days and weeks fall into a predictable shape.

The drive to Silverdown became automatic, as if the car could almost take itself. Often I was so deep in my thoughts that I hardly remembered getting there. Little things grew in importance, like the soft toy dogs. I arrived one day to find Eddie happily tucked up under his blanket in the day room, nursing a small toy St Bernard puppy. He was patting and stroking it, treating it like a real dog. 'He's a grand lad,' said Eddie. 'No trouble. We better take him for a walk later.' We agreed this was a good idea but we'd hang on until it stopped raining.

For the next few days, whenever I arrived Eddie would be chatting to and cuddling 'his dog'. He called it Misty, after his old sheepdog who'd died just before we were married. If it wasn't on his knee it was on the chair beside him, and was quite often offered tit-bits at tea time. The toy had a beautiful face; they make such lovely soft toys these days. There were a few other toys around, mostly dogs, the odd cat and some teddy bears. Other patients had their favourites and were often seen holding them. There was also a medium sized baby-doll, dressed and wrapped in baby blankets. Some of the elderly women treated this as a real child to be rocked and comforted with coos and singing. The doll was always handled with great care, as one would handle a baby, gently dressed and undressed, its nappy changed then settled back into a box or on a chair.

Ivy had a large dark-blue shopping bag on wheels to avoid carrying heavy items. She was always busy pushing it around, quite often bumping it into chairs and tables but rarely into people. I would watch her stuffing anything that took her fancy into the bag: newspapers, cups and saucers, any discarded clothing plus a good selection of soft toys would vanish into the depths of her bag. The carers warned me not to leave anything unattended if she was on the prowl as she could become very agitated if they tried to take anything from her.

One day I made the mistake of turning my back on my handbag, only to see it disappearing into Ivy's treasure chest. Now the bargaining had to begin as one of the staff chatted to her about the contents of her shopping bag. 'Have you got any washing in there, needs doing?' Ivy didn't think so, but was persuaded to open it. Various items, including my bag, were hauled out. Missing spectacles, a couple of lost cardigans and fluffy teddies and dogs appeared. 'You won't be wanting this bag,' said the carer, trying to disentangle my handbag from the hoard.

'Mine!' said Ivy, making a grab. By now it was on her shoulder and she was clutching it with grim determination. I was getting ready to go, wondering how on earth they would retrieve it. This minor drama passed Eddie by; he was busy feeding a piece of biscuit to Misty. The situation was salvaged when the nurse turned up holding her own bag. 'You have this one, Ivy. That one's a bit small to fit in all your bits.'

Ivy slipped my bag from her shoulder and considered the exchange. Resting it on a nearby table, she proceeded to empty out the contents, inspecting each item in detail. Purse, hairbrush, comb, mirror, handkerchief, notebook and pen, they rolled around as she sorted through. I was thankful I wasn't in the habit of carrying anything like a spare pair of knickers.

'Here, you take this bag,' said the nurse.

Ivy gave it a suspicious look then grudgingly took it. She was busy inspecting it as I crammed everything back into mine and made a dash for the exit. Suddenly, realising she'd been duped, Ivy raised an angry head. Yelling, 'Thief, she's stolen my handbag,' she rushed after me.

Two of the staff managed to keep hold of her as I got through the door. My last vision of Silverdown that day was of Ivy frantically hammering with her fists on the inside of the glass entrance door, screaming, 'Thief! Thief!'

A day or two later I arrived and rapidly realised that all the soft toys had vanished. Surely they couldn't all be in Ivy's bag? Or had she taken them back to her room? On enquiring, to my dismay I was told they'd been sorted by the night staff; most had been sent to be destroyed and a few had gone to the laundry.

I couldn't say much because it had obviously been done for good reasons. Infections could spread easily in an environment where 'the wanderers' shared each other's belongings and had less than perfect hygiene habits.

It was the first time for a number of days that I'd seen Eddie without Misty. His hands strayed over and under his blanket as he hunted for the dog. We had morning coffee and biscuits and we looked through his horse picture book.

Thankfully, Felix turned up. She made her way around the patients, spending time on Ron's knee before moving onto Eddie. There she settled for a while, Eddie gently stroking the black-and-white fur as she purred. But Felix always shared herself out and before long she was on her way over to Jessie.

FELIX

She moved in with Harry years ago
but when he died, would not be denied her home,
each time they carried her away
she returned, so they let her stay.
She is a study in serenity,
as sunlight over sea
she strolls around the home observing,
purring softly, seeking knees,
she aims to please and comfort all.
Anyone can tote her round,
most days she's found
padding peacefully from chair to chair,
she seems to really care,
never judges, holds no grudges if pulled and poked,
always forgives,

welcomes unsure hands, and hugs.
She comes on silent feet,
sleek, she tours the carpet round 'her family',
to her they are the same,
they remain
    the people that they were.

I stayed until after lunch. Eddie had lost a small amount of weight and the staff had told me he was becoming difficult at meal times, only eating a little and saying he was full. I encouraged him to eat but he soon pushed it away. What he did eat was recorded. 'Don't worry,' they assured me. 'We're watching him carefully and someone sits with him at each meal. We also hand out chocolate and treats during the day.'

When I left him he was dozing fitfully, his hands still roving around the blanket feeling for Misty.

I managed to reach the car before I started to cry. Why take all the soft toys at one go? Couldn't they have left a few? Where was Misty? Would he come back clean from the laundry or was he heading for the dump or incinerator? In the scale of things, it sounds ridiculous to howl over a toy St Bernard but to Eddie it had become Misty. I remembered a story I'd read, how a toy rabbit was loved so much it became real. That toy, as far as Eddie was concerned, was the genuine article; it was his old dog returned to love and comfort him, and now it was gone. I determined to do what I could to help, so I went on a 'soft-toy dog hunt'.

I drove into town and started on the charity shops. I had considered the market and toy shops, but decided that there was little point in buying something expensive because the toys had a limited life at Silverdown. Also, hopefully a troll round the charity shops might produce a number of toys for the collective price of a new one.

Like many high streets these days, there was a selection of good, clean charity shops. At each one I headed for the toys. Tiny ones were of no use; they had to be of a decent size to cuddle, with soft, tactile fur and happy, loving faces. I drew a blank at the first shop but in the second I found a miniature Old English sheepdog. He was lovely, not too large, and with the most adorable face.

'Buying for the grandchildren?' the pleasant volunteer behind the counter asked.

I could have just said yes, but the shop wasn't busy and perhaps I needed to talk.

'No it's for my husband. He has vascular dementia and he thinks toy dogs are real.' Poor woman, I thought as I spoke, she's most likely got a pile of her own troubles. Why burden her with mine? I needn't have worried.

'How sad that must be,' she said. 'My husband died of cancer four years ago, so I know what you're going through. Life can be cruel.' As she chatted, she found a bag for the dog. 'Do you want any more?'

'Yes, if there's anything similar. I can share them out around the other patients.' She disappeared into the back room and returned shortly holding three more similar-sized dogs. One was black, one golden like a Labrador, and the other a black-and-white collie.

'Will these do?' They were perfect. We settled on a pound each and, laden down with bags of dogs, I headed for the car.

This was to be the first of many 'dog' excursions. I became obsessed and found it difficult to pass a charity shop without a rummage through their soft toys. I found dogs of every size and colour, with gentle eyes, soft noses and generous smiles. They all found their way to Silverdown to be cuddled, dragged around, shoved into Ivy's bag, covered in rice pudding, tea or urine, but most of all to bring comfort and love. Since the toys did vanish at regular intervals, I always had a stock at home and kept a spare one in Eddie's wardrobe to bring out when needed. He was never dogless again.

I presented him with the Old English sheepdog the next morning. Misty Number Two was immediately accepted and tucked under his blanket. The other dogs were shared out. Soon Ron was stroking the Labrador, the black fluffy dog was carried off by Jessie and the other was fought over by two patients before eventually being pushed under a chair when they lost interest before it was scooped up by Ivy.

I settled down with Eddie. Having given Misty a good pat, he decided that we should find some scissors and cut the hair from around its eyes. 'The poor old thing can't see where he's going,' Eddie complained. 'How can he get about with all that hair over his eyes?' He spent most of the next hour picking at the fur around Misty's eyes. I resolved to bring scissors next day and have a chopping session if it was still bothering him.

In early January there was 'conference day' when Eddie's case was reviewed. This involved Rachel (Eddie's social worker), Nurse Maggie, Carol and myself. The object of the conference was to see how Eddie had settled and assess his general care and behaviour since admission. Carol had the Silverdown records, which were kept meticulously each day and night to give a full picture, and his care plan.

It was the general feeling that Eddie had settled well and was as content and happy as his condition allowed. He'd had a few falls and was on special observation if he moved; also his weight loss was causing concern. Everything he ate and drank was recorded and he'd been prescribed supplements, plus he was being weighed weekly. It had been noted that increasingly he was becoming doubly incontinent. There had been a few psychotic incidents during the night, but the staff had managed to calm him down with a one-to-one chat and warm drinks. Apart from his normal medication, he was never given any form of sedation; they didn't agree with 'the medicinal cosh' at Silverdown.

I came away from the conference knowing I'd made the correct decision. The twenty-four hour care he was receiving was much better than one worn-out woman could have provided. No matter how much home assistance had been offered, he would never have had the total care maintenance he was now receiving. Love can do only so much; there comes a point that love brims over into selfishness. There is a narrow defining line between caring for someone for their sake and for your own.

This knowledge that I'd done the right thing, for the right reason, in no way diminished the feeling of guilt that would always be there; that's the paradox, to feel both vindicated and guilty at the same time.

Sunday 8th January. Eddie is still in bed when I arrive at 10am, he's snug under his duvet and woolly blanket but on inspection I realise he's wet, so I tell the staff and they come to get him up. 'We tried to rouse him earlier but he was having none of it, we'll soon have him sorted out,' says one of the carers.

I wait in the day room. About twenty minutes later, I see them walking him up the corridor from his room. It takes the two carers to steady him, his legs are very wobbly today. They settle him down on a chair next to me and tea and chocolate biscuits soon appear, they know those are his favourite.

He says it's good to see me here but it's been ages. I smile and say I'm sorry – he's forgotten I spent most of yesterday with him. He's not really sure where here is but later he's talking about the farm and village, so I suppose we must be at home. He chats about villagers and farmers he knows, especially Arty and Craig.

Jessie walks past. She's a tiny woman, barely five foot, with straight grey hair and awful varicose veins. She's in a bad mood today and scowls at my smile. 'That woman spends her whole day walking about,' says Eddie.

'Perhaps she's lost something.'

'I wish she'd damn well find it!' he answers.

Later he wants the toilet. One of the male carers takes him but Audrey's bagged it, she's in and out all day. 'Get out!' she screams. 'I'm in here.'

'Eddie's desperate,' says the carer, keeping a tight hold of the swaying Eddie. Audrey vacates, muttering, and heads for the other room where she meets Jessie. They collide and battle commences. The staff rush to separate them. Jessie manages to kick Audrey's ankle before stamping off. Audrey informs the world she's been attacked and the duty nurse attends with cream and a bandage, though there's little sign of injury,

Eddie's back and we look through his picture book. I've bought a new one with lovely pictures of Cumbria. I point out places we've visited. Sometimes he seems to remember, at others he just nods and smiles.

I mention my friend Pauline is still in Australia. We're immediately transported in his mind and we're on a plane.

'How long is the flight?' Eddie asks.

''Thirty hours.'

'I don't fancy that, let's go somewhere else.'

'That's fine by me. Where do you want to go?'

He's pondering as Jessie wanders by; she's shouting about something.

'She's a bad passenger,' says Eddie. 'They'll have to put her off.'

'Perhaps she's scared,' I say.

Eddie shakes his head. 'She's just daft.' (Daft was becoming his favourite form of expression for anything of which he disapproved.)

Maisie comes and stands in front of us. As usual her cardigan is buttoned up wrongly, and her face holds an anguished expression. 'Hell! Hell!' she growls as she turns away up the corridor.

Ivy walks by and stops. 'I'm going home,' she tells me, gripping her wheely bag.'

'That's grand,' I say.

'I've tried all the doors but they're locked. What time's the bus?'

'After lunch,' I answer. This mollifies her and she walks away, heading for the bus stop.

Eddie's nodding off and it's nearly lunchtime. 'Are you going to wake up for something to eat?' I ask, he nods his head but his eyes remain closed.

Sam comes and hovers over us. 'It's like this,' he says, frustrated, pointing to his palm. 'You have to press here, and then open and close it. That works.'

'Good, I'm glad you've solved it.'

He's gone but Ivy is back. 'Are you somebody called Digby?' she asks.

'No, pet,' I assure her. She tuts, disgusted, and goes off to ask someone else.

Lunch is served; today it's turkey with mashed potatoes and sprouts. I cut up Eddie's turkey and he tucks in quietly. He eats about half then pushes it away, but does better with the rice pudding.

Maisie is stalking down the corridor clutching a jug of water. She throws it at a wall – luckily the jug is plastic and bounces. She continues to the door and stands there kicking it. Eddie, eating his rice pudding, is unaware as Audrey limps by still complaining about being attacked.

Jessie is on her rounds again, closing doors, opening doors, gathering up cups and cursing anyone who comes near. Ron turns up, he's walking out of the dining room clutching a bowl of rice. He heads our way and drops a spoonful down Eddie's chair. Eddie doesn't notice. I mop up as Ron wanders off dispensing spoonfuls of rice in little piles on the carpet. One of the carers tries to take the bowl away. Ron laughs and throws the last spoonful at her.

Eddie says he's enjoyed his lunch. He's done quite well today. I drag Misty from under his chair and he wraps his arms around it. Maisie's back again and makes a grab for Misty, but Eddie holds on tight, and the nurse leads her away.

Eddie rests his chin on Misty, his eyes close and he sleeps, nestled beneath his blanket, content in his own strange world. Because this is where we are: me, Eddie, Maisie, Jessie, Ivy, Sam, Ron and all the others caught in this bizarre world. The patients remain the people they were; outwardly many look unchanged apart from natural ageing, but dementia has torn their minds. They exist in a land of their own imagining, at times more lucid than others. The pieces of their lives, their fragmented memories, are still there but buried, thrown into turmoil by the ravages of the illness.

I pull on my coat, kiss Eddie and head for the main door. Outside the world goes on unchanged. A train rushes by in the distance, a car arrives bringing more relatives, they pass me crunching over the white chippings. I reach the car. It's starting to rain.

***

Quite often when I visited, Eddie was up but asleep in his

chair. Increasingly he would be hidden under his blanket, which completely enveloped him. I'd peep underneath. 'Are you coming out to say hello, Eddie?' I'd ask. Many times there would be no response apart from a hand grasping the blanket, drawing it closer. Sometimes he would be grumpy at being disturbed and the hand would come towards me, wrapped in blanket, to push me away.

So I would sit there, hemmed in this world, watching, listening and thinking. The staff were always kind and solicitous, bringing me a tray of tea and biscuits or cake. The minutes would tick away, turn into an hour.

While Eddie Sleeps

Jessie closes doors,
Ron walks around unspeaking,
Maisie stares at space,
chews a finger, swears,
Sam ambles by looking for escape,
Jessie opens doors,
stacks magazines,
Len starts to cry,
Is comforted, calms, but cries again,
cheers up, smiles,
plays with his furry toy,
as Jessie closes doors.
Sam curls up to a carer,
rests his head,
Ron totters by, moaning,
Jessie opens doors,
Maisie churns her cardigan,
walks on to nowhere,
Len hammers on the wall,

then demands a shave,
as Eddie sleeps
Jessie closes doors.

Saturday 21st January, 7.30am, the phone rang. Eddie's been wandering around since 3.30am. They thought they'd settled him but he got up again and had a tumble. He's okay, the nurse assures me, but he's grazed his head. I thank her for the call. They know to phone me if anything out of the ordinary happens.

I arrive to see him at 10.30. He has a small plaster on his forehead but seems none the worse. We chat about how busy he's been that morning; he's had a cow cut a teat and the vet's due. 'Damn typical,' he says. 'It would be one of the good milkers, never some old girl past her best. She'll get mastitis next.' We bemoan the state of farming and the many problems involved with keeping stock.

The duty nurse comes over to check Eddie's alright after the fall. She consults the night report. 'He fell forward before they could reach him.' She gently takes the plaster off; there's a small wound underneath, which has bled a little. 'Is your head sore, Eddie?' she asks.

'No, I've had worse than this,' he assures her. 'I was trying to fluke a cow and I got a bang. Be better in no time.' Smiling, she applies a fresh plaster.

It was the next day, and I was getting ready to visit, when I had another telephone call. This time it was to say that a few of the patients had gone down with a vomiting and diarrhoea bug; for the time being they were asking visitors to stay away. There was quite a lot of this going round the area, and I knew a few people who'd been ill, so it didn't surprise me that it had got into Silverdown. The staff tried but, with the patients wandering around, sharing the same space, toilets and property, at times it was an almost impossible task to keep germs at bay.

I enquired about Eddie. He was fine, he'd had a better night, no further falls and the graze wasn't bothering him. They were still concerned he wasn't eating well but that was being closely monitored. They'd let me know as soon as visitors were allowed and I could phone any time.

I didn't know then but it would be more than two weeks, Monday 6th February, before I was to see Eddie again as the bug gripped Silverdown. Each day there were new cases; thankfully Eddie kept clear, but I worried all the time. Already being incontinent, he had enough to cope with; if he developed uncontrollable diarrhoea as well, he could become really ill.

I phoned daily but, as the days slipped away, I became more and more desperate to see him. Outside the weather was atrocious and very cold. I would lie in bed at night, hoping Eddie was warm enough – he felt the cold so badly now. Had he got his blanket? Was he being dressed in his warm clothes? Was he eating? Did he still have Misty, or had all the soft toys been swept away as health hazards? The questions and worries never eased. I was always assured when I rang that all was well and I did trust them, I had to, but it wasn't the same as being there and seeing for myself.

As the days stretched, my guilt stretched with them. If he'd stayed at home, he'd have been protected from infections passed around a care home. I kept reliving the past months: should I have done this or not have done that? Why hadn't I the strength to cope? Had I given up too easily? I tortured myself with questions.

I found it almost impossible to concentrate on anything, each day going through the motions of life. I'd go to the shop, see people. 'How are you?' they'd ask. 'Fine,' I'd answer, with a slapped-on smile. Invariably the next question was, 'How's Eddie?' My stock reply was, 'Unchanged, but I can't visit at the moment. They've got a bug at Silverdown.'

I'd walk away. I couldn't help wondering what they were really thinking. How many of them blamed me for 'putting him in a home', the worse thing anyone can do to a loved one?

On the 5th February it snowed. The snow hung like blossom on trees and bushes. Roofs and wall tops were layered with a cloak of white, just like a Christmas card. I went to church but was too choked-up to linger in conversation and was glad to get home. Thankfully, when I phoned the following morning, I was given the all clear and with relief, I jumped in the car and sped off. The snow lingered on the fields but the roads were clear so I had little trouble getting to Silverdown.

Eddie was sitting in the day room, well wrapped up in jumpers and a blanket. His face lit up as he saw me. I settled beside him and he took my hand. For the first few minutes he said little, just stroking my palm, running his work-rough fingers up and down, round and round.

When he started to talk, he said it was strange living at The Mill without me and hoped I'd enjoyed my holiday. 'You're always off somewhere these days,' he added. 'Where've you been this time?' Somehow I held on to my emotions as I assured him I'd only been to see his Ruby.

Happy that Ruby was okay, he said he wanted to take me out. 'Somewhere nice, since I haven't seen you for such a long time.'

I tried to console myself with the thought that he said this even when I'd been coming daily. I told him that was a lovely idea but it was a cold outside today, and could we wait until it was a bit warmer. This put his mind at ease, especially when I presented him with Misty Number Three, or was it Four or Five? I'd lost count. He was soon cuddling it, stroking its ears, and saying what a 'grand dog' it was.

I'd been there barely an hour when one of the carers came over. They'd just discovered two new cases of 'the bug' and all visitors were being asked to leave. I told Eddie I was off to make lunch, kissed him and slipped away.

I met Arthur as I left; his wife had been in Silverdown for a number of years. Before the quarantine, he'd come twice a day, every day, to see her. He was very distressed as he left, saying he wasn't sleeping and the separation was torment. I knew exactly how he felt. Luckily, on this occasion it was a false alarm and visitors were allowed back a couple of days later.

February slipped unnoticed into March and life went on. Eddie's weight loss had made him look old and boney. The staff and I did everything we could to encourage him to eat. Some days he did better than others, porridge, rice pudding and custard remaining his favourites. I often stayed for lunch, keeping him going when he decided he was full. 'Just another mouthful,' I'd say, and to please me he might try a little more. But on many occasions no amount of encouragement worked and he would push his plate away after a few bites. The carers would ask him what he fancied; at times jelly, ice cream or chocolate became a substitute for lunch. It didn't matter as long as he was eating something.

As the weeks wore on Eddie became more and more sleepy; on many visits he would sleep the whole time I was there. Often he was still in bed when I arrived, having refused to get up earlier. The staff would check him every fifteen minutes to see if he'd woken. Silverdown had a 'patients do what they wish' policy. No one was forced to get up until they were ready, then they would be washed, dressed and brought into the day room. Turning this on its head, patients could wander out of their rooms any time they wished, be it three o'clock in the morning, and they could return to bed when they decided.

This meant each day was unpredictable. Sometimes Eddie would be wide awake having morning tea and chocolate biscuits when I arrived, and we would chatter on for an hour. Other days I would sit by his bed waiting for him to wake, or sit beside him in the day room as he slept.

March 2012 was unseasonably warm and on the 29th it was hot enough to pass for June. Having been built for dementia patients, Silverdown had a safe, enclosed garden. This was a lovely area with flowers, grass, seats and tables surrounded by sheltering trees. On fine days, the patients were encouraged to go out. They were always well-chaperoned by the carers, especially the ones like Eddie who were prone to falls.

The 29th was a Thursday. After Eddie had been helped into a garden chair, we sat together enjoying the sunshine. It was digestive biscuits today and Eddie sat, happily dunking them in his tea as we chatted. That day he was obsessed by builders for some reason. 'They've been busy all week,' he assured me, as a carer walked by. 'How's the wall coming on?' he asked. 'Must make sure it's sound enough to keep the cows in.' Then he changed tack. 'You have to watch them. Take you to the cleaners if you're not careful.'

His dunked biscuit vanished into his tea and he played around trying to catch it. 'They wanted to cut these trees down but we wouldn't let them,' he laughed. 'A whole gang of us, we stood in front and kept them off. They're not knocking down my trees, they give shade for the cows in this weather.'

On Tuesday April 1st, I'd been asked to attend a special

review of Eddie's case at the home. There was a nursing representative from Silverdown who had all Eddie's notes, a social worker and a nurse representing the NHS. I didn't realise how important this meeting was, thinking it was just routine. Every aspect of Eddie's condition was discussed and all the available information brought together. I said little unless I was asked a question, mainly listening as they talked.

Mobility, difficulty with food and appetite, risk of falls, cognition, blackouts, medication, communication skills and other aspects of his case were explored in detail. I hadn't known how disturbed he'd been at times during the night, and how much one-to-one care he'd needed and received. As I listened, it was brought home to me vividly how much he'd deteriorated and what little chance I would have had trying to cope at home.

Each element of his care plan was scored. He was classified as severe in one section, high in six sections, moderate in six and low in only one. To my amazement, the NHS nurse turned to me and, with the agreement of the social worker, informed me that they were going to make a recommendation that Eddie be awarded full NHS funding.

I had no idea this was available. It was called Continuing NHS Care, and was only awarded if his score classification met the criteria. The nurse said that she must now prepare a thirty-five-page case document, with photocopied evidence from Eddie's file, and this would have to be presented to a panel for approval. She couldn't guarantee the funding would be forthcoming but, with all three of those present signing off on it, there was a strong chance it would go through. I would be notified in two weeks.

My head was in a whirl as I drove away from Silverdown. If it was approved, I need no longer worry about funding. I tried not to build up my hopes in case it was turned down but, if it was granted, it meant that when Eddie's share of our savings diminished, I need not worry about having to sell the land.

EASTER 2012

Easter, the days have tumbled from November,
he's shrunk since then,
sunk inwards,
bunched small,
sliding slowly to oblivion.
He nurses fluffy toys,
calls them friends,
he bends into his chair,
cannot grasp that I am there.
His paper-skin wrinkles,
rubber lips fold up,
I know not what he thinks,
as he sinks.
He looks so old today,
the Easter Bunny laughs,
then hops away.

On the 16th, I was asked to go into the office when I arrived at Silverdown. The panel had granted the Continuing Care funding, which would be backdated. Was I wrong to feel so relieved? Was I being mercenary? I had to tell myself it had been granted because of the severity of Eddie's condition; it was only what he was entitled to. In a strange way I also felt guilt mixed in with the relief. There would be a review in three months and after that the funding was assured for a year. We often decry the NHS but when it works well, it is wonderful.

CHAPTER 10

MEMORIES

The 29th of April 2012 was our thirty-sixth wedding anniversary. In all those years, Eddie had never failed to give me a card. I'd told the staff a few days before and they'd bought one for him to sign. The signature was almost illegible – he could no longer write – but the card was waiting on the table when I arrived at 11.30.

He was deeply asleep, cuddled up under blankets in his chair, the latest Misty, a collie, cradled in his arms. It was no good: when I saw him I just couldn't stop crying. Every time I gathered a little composure, back came the tears.

The staff were wonderful and one of the carers, who I knew really well by now, took me in the office and let me howl all over her. Tea and sympathy did help as we chatted and I told her about our wedding day and the honeymoon we'd spent in North Wales. We both started laughing as I described our day at Blackrock Sands near Porthmadog when the car got stuck in the sinking sand and was nearly swept out by the tide.

'It was getting dusk and the sea was only a few feet away. Poor Eddie was digging round the wheels as if he were off to Australia but the car wouldn't budge. Then I spied some fishermen in the distance and dashed off for help. They were four big, strapping chaps and they literally lifted the car out of the sand, then pushed us on our way. But it was a near-do.

Fancy nearly losing our car in the sea on our honeymoon!'

Eddie woke up around noon and we had lunch together. He was eating a little better and had recovered a tiny amount of weight. Afterwards we sat on a couch in the day room looking through the wedding album, which I'd brought with me. I wasn't sure how much he remembered but he kept nodding and smiling as I turned the pages, now and again pointing to various people he recognised.

An elderly gentleman came to entertain in the afternoon, playing his clarinet. They often managed to get musicians to come to the home. They played tunes that the residents might remember, and we would have a sing-song. The residents would all be assembled on comfy chairs for the performance; though some went to sleep, or wandered off, there were others who sang or hummed along, memories of the past awoken again by the well-known melodies.

As the clarinettist played and we tucked into afternoon tea and cake, Eddie was transported to a wedding. 'I'm so glad we were invited,' he said. 'Is that the bride?' He pointed to one of the residents sitting the other side of the room. She was wearing a white blouse, which became her wedding dress. 'She's a bit long in the tooth,' he added, 'but she looks happy. This wedding cake is lovely, and he's a grand entertainer.'

I left around four and went to see Pauline. Not for the first or final time, I sobbed all over her. We went down to the service station for an evening meal and had a chat, which made me feel better. I was glad when the day was over, but found that sleep escaped me until the early hours.

I was not, of course, Eddie's only visitor. Arty, our farming friend who had been so helpful when we were struggling at home, popped in fairly frequently, and others came with me, especially Pauline. Family and neighbours went occasionally, but I think all of them were so deeply affected by the change in Eddie that they found it very difficult to go too often.

I can understand how they felt. Not only had they to overcome the charged atmosphere of the dementia home, which could be intimidating and distressing, but they had to try and make conversation with a man who was a shadow of the person they knew, both physically and mentally. Those he had known the longest faired the best because his recollections of his younger life were still fairly coherent, but with others he would nod with his usual smile, believing them to be strangers. 'I don't think he really remembered us,' they would say after a visit. I didn't blame them for not returning.

On May 9th I went away for a two-day painting holiday in the Lake District. I'd really agonised about going, feeling there was no way I should be enjoying myself while Eddie was in Silverdown. I'd already discovered, during the enforced quarantine spell, that he sometimes missed me when I couldn't visit, but he'd also forget I'd been, even if I'd hardly missed a day for weeks. I realised this short break would be no different. Silverdown had my mobile number and the address and phone number of where I was staying. Should anything happen, I could be back in just over an hour. All this logic and preparation didn't lessen the guilt.

Pauline, who is a talented watercolour artist, was running the course at a well- appointed hotel. It was a lovely few days, so relaxing, with good company, lots of laughs. Though I'm no artist, I managed to produce one fairly good painting. I found, as I immersed my mind in the paint, that just for a short while the mental pain and worry slipped away as I became lost in brush strokes and the art of creation.

So strange, this change to be absorbed in paint,
to sink into a landscape,

awake blank paper with a brush,
tease texture into bark,
conjure mountains with a touch,
add ripples to a lake –
and for a little while,
relax and smile.

Predictably, Eddie was fine when I went to see him shortly after my return. He was in a chatty mood in the day room and spoke to me as if I'd just been out of the room for a few minutes. We had a contented afternoon together, looking through one of his horse books and another book with scenic local views. This meant I could talk about places we'd visited. I know he didn't always remember but he'd press a finger to the page. 'Pretty.'

I had an especially bad day the following Sunday. As I headed to Silverdown, I started trembling, an awful dread of the place sweeping over me. I felt as if I were drowning and could bear it no longer. Perhaps it was because of the break and having relaxed. I forced myself to keep driving, turn into the car park, get out of the car, and walk to the entrance. I signed in, spoke into the intercom and was soon inside. It was around 2pm. I'd started to go in the afternoon more often, as there was a better chance of him being alert and awake. Today was to prove the exception.

I looked around the day room but he wasn't there.

'Eddie's in his room,' said one of the carers. 'He was up and about this morning from five. He's had lunch and gone back to his room. He didn't want to go to bed, so we sat him in his chair. I looked in a few minutes ago and he was dozing.'

I headed for his room, using my key to get in. Eddie was propped up with cushions in his easy chair, a blanket round his knees, deeply asleep. The chair was against the bed, where his latest toy dog rested. It was a miniature Labrador with a kind face, and it truly seemed to be watching him. The staff had put on his radio, which was playing a piece of beautiful classical music, a real haunting tune which I know well but can't name. I sat beside him, pondering on the present, remembering the past.

He woke an hour later. After a toilet call, the staff walked him through into the day room where we shared afternoon tea. I left around four, driving home on automatic pilot, not aware of my surroundings until I reached home. It's a wonder I was never caught speeding in the intervening villages as I drove through them so many times with no memory of the drive.

As I turned into the lane, I had this great horror of the empty house. I needed someone to hold on to, tell them how I felt and most likely cry again, but Pauline was away at her son's. Other friends always had family on a Sunday and anyway everyone had their own sadness and worries. Why should I inflict my despair onto them? So I went home, hugged the cats, made a cup of tea and watched telly. Life went on; as Scarlett O'Hara said, 'Tomorrow is another day.'

One afternoon I had one of the most surreal conversations ever. I'd just arrived and sat down next to Eddie, whose head was covered with his fleece-lined blanket. He peeped round. 'Have you got the water on?' he asked.

Realising he was back on the farm and we were due to wash the milk bottles, I said yes. That satisfied him and he vanished back under the blanket.

Elsie walked towards us and pulled up a chair. She was a fairly new resident and always asking when she could go home. I always felt desperately sorry for her elderly husband when he came to visit as she would cling onto him, begging him not to go and to take her home.

'Hallo, lady,' she said. 'What's your name?'

'Jackie.'

'My name's Elsie. Where are we?'

'Silverdown.'

'Where do you live?'

'In a small village,' I said.

'I live on a farm.'

Just then Jessie turned up, standing over us, very agitated. 'I blame the government,' she said, her face screwed in anger. 'The gardener wants to do his work but the government won't let him.'

I nodded in agreement as Eddie's head came from under the blanket.

'Have you put the water on?'

'Yes' I assured him. 'It will be ready soon.'

Again he retreated, again came Elsie's inquiry. 'What's your name?'

'Jackie.'

'My name's Elsie. Where are we?'

'Silverdown.'

'Where do you live?'

'In a small village.'

Jessie stamped her foot. 'It's the damn government. That poor gardener, why can't they let him get on with his work?'

'Where are we?' asked Elsie.

'Have you put that water on?' asked Eddie.

'It's the government!!' yelled Jessie, 'I blame the government.' And so it went on, round and round, a record stuck in this groove.

The days, weeks and months slipped away, spring turned to summer. My birthday came and went, unnoticed by Eddie for the first time since our marriage. I didn't remind him;

there seemed no point.

The day was made bearable by the love and support of friends. I spent the morning at the home, was treated to afternoon tea at Pat's and taken by Pauline to the theatre for the evening.

As on so many occasions, it turned out to be an unsettled summer: lots of rain, cold at times, with intermittent days of blissful heat. When I wasn't at Silverdown, I kept busy. It was the only way to cope. I never went anywhere without my mobile phone so I was always reachable should the need arise.

One day I was shopping in town and went into a café for lunch. Alone, I soon plunged deep into thought, mulling over the recent months, worrying about the future. I finished, stood up and left, wandering aimlessly down the street. I heard running footsteps behind me; I'd left without paying and the waitress had chased after me. I felt awful. Thankfully she accepted my apologies as, extremely embarrassed, I returned to pay.

I found at times, when I was in good company and enjoying WI events or village activities, that for a short while I didn't think about Eddie. But when the realisation hit me again, the guilt redoubled that I had dared to pass an hour without him constantly on my mind. It felt inexcusable to laugh and go about normal day-to-day life, as if I had committed a terrible sin by not being constantly unhappy. My love for him never lessened; it wasn't as if I didn't care – God, how I cared – but surely it must be wrong to be enjoying myself, while he sat in the home being looked after by strangers, huddled under a blanket as his mind and existence slowly slipped away?

June saw the Queen's Jubilee celebrations in London. My friend Wendy was going; it was a once-in-a-lifetime event.

In my opinion, I now committed an even greater sin because I went with her. Right up to the day before travelling I felt I shouldn't be going, but the Silverdown staff assured me I was right to go. I would only be away a few days; I could phone each day to make sure he was okay and if anything unexpected occurred I could be on the next train home. So I went.

Yes, I was packed in with the thousands, cheering our hearts out in the rain on the banks of the Thames as the Jubilee Parade of boats sailed past. I was five-deep back from the river, watching through one of these periscope contraptions. I would have seen much more on the telly but the atmosphere was amazing. I did see the Queen the next day as her car headed for St Paul's, and later I waved my flag frantically just off The Mall, and saw the back of her car. But I was there and I'll never forget the experience.

I rushed off to see Eddie as soon as I came home. He'd been fine, never noticed my absence, and spoke to me as if I'd just popped into the kitchen to make a cup of tea.

> I've been to London, to see the Jubilee
> and just returned today,
> but I might have never been away.
> His eyes slipped into mine.
> He has not pined,
> nor missed my smile,
> I could have been a step
> or thousand miles,
> he would not know,
> it must be so.

Eddie's talkative days became increasingly infrequent, to be enjoyed when they occurred. Then we would range over a vast array of muddled-up subjects. If we spoke of sheep, before I knew it he would have launched into a rambling tale about having spent the morning chasing these escaped sheep round our land.

'Damn things!' he would complain. Eddie was a cow man and he had little time or patience with sheep. 'They've been getting over that wall in the top field. It was a bit damaged but you should see it now – they've dislodged all the top. I managed to get them cornered but I had a hell of a job getting them back through the gate. I could have done with the old dog. Where is she?' I knew he was talking about his last sheepdog, Misty, who had been dead more than thirty years.

'She was asleep down near the house.'

'Lazy old girl,' Eddie laughed. 'Anyway I managed at last and I've spent the rest of the day putting the wall back up, though it's not my wall. The chap in the next field won't repair it.' Then we would be into walls and walling until we would jump on to another unconnected subject.

Sometimes he would start to struggle up from his chair. I'd grab him as he swayed and a carer would hurry over. 'I've got to be off for the cows,' he'd protest, trying to disentangle himself. 'It'll soon be milking time and that good milker's got a touch of mastitis. She needs another tube in her tit or she'll loose that quarter.'

Then we would walk, a carer supporting him each side. Eddie tottered along, his once-strong gait a weak shuffle. Up and down the corridor, me wandering behind, Eddie calling as he had so often to the cows, 'Cush! Cush!

'Cush! Cush!'
I see you still, the cows ambling ahead,
'Cush! Cush!' you said,

and they would graze almost unaware
that you were there.
'Cush! Cush!' you'd gentle them along,
with your morning, evening song
called through all weathers,
under sun or thrashing rain,
'Cush! Cush!' you'd call again.

I see you still, the tractor trembling by
watching sky,
or walling gaps.
Perhaps on a dreamy day of soaking sun,
you'd pause from work,
hum one of your inane tunes
where no music ever went,
but you were so content.

I see you still, both boy and man,
your land was part of you, since you began,
the miles you must have trod
as seasons scurried on,
the land remains, but you are gone.

'Cush! Cush!' the words come back
before the calling breeze,
they frame your face,
speak your name in leafless trees,
I ache to see your smile again today,
It seems a long time, since we walked this way

One day in July, I arrived to find Eddie very sombre.
'Shush!' he whispered. 'They're just carrying the coffin in.' We
were at a funeral; I never discovered whose. We had to stand

as the bearers carried in the body. 'Did you buy the flowers?' asked Eddie. I assured him that I had, then suddenly the funeral became a wedding and we were throwing confetti, Eddie was asking if his suit was okay and commenting on how nice the bride looked.

We went on to talk about weddings as he tucked into a bar of chocolate. I asked him who he married.

'Oh, she was a nice lass.'

'What was she called?' I asked.

His face creased in thought. He licked his lips, savouring the chocolate, sucking his fingers as they became sticky. 'I don't really remember,' he paused, searching for the answer. 'I know – Mary.'

'How about Jackie?'

'Oh, I knew her once for a short while, but that was a long time ago. She was a nice lass as well.'

'Who is Jackie?'
'I used to know,
but that was long ago.'
'Did you have a wife?'
'Yes, in some other life.'
'What was her name?'
(should I explain?)
'Was it Mary?
I'm not sure.'
Another door is closed –
'Who is Jackie?'

I was to find that this was not an isolated incident; increasingly Eddie wasn't really sure who I was. He called me by different names, mainly Ruby or Mary. I struggled not to let it upset me. I'd known it was coming, it wasn't a surprise.

July sped away. In London the Olympics were in full swing. I'm not really a sports fan; I like a bit of tennis and horse racing and, when I was in my teens, I used to go and watch Manchester United. Eddie, unlike most men, had never been particularly interested in sport. Over the last few years we'd enjoyed watching Formula One motor racing on the telly and the occasional football match. I did watch the Olympic opening ceremony, which was unbelievable: so clever, such vision to be able to create what they did. After that I saw far more of the events than I expected, glowing with pride at the many achievements of our competitors.

I also couldn't help thinking that, if things hadn't turned out as they had, Eddie and I would certainly have spent a few days in London. Like the Jubilee, this was a once-in-a-lifetime chance to see the Olympics on home turf and I know we wouldn't have missed the chance.

Eddie's sleepiness was increasing all the time when I went to visit. On so many occasions I tried unsuccessfully to wake him. He would either mutter something and pull his blanket up over his head or push me away. Then I would sit, either holding his hand or just watching as the time ticked away, like his life was also ticking away. One way to control the welling thoughts and emotions was to write.

Friday 13th
I eat biscuits, drink tea,
this is me inside this nightmare,
he lies there in his chair,
lost in sleep,
a fluffy toy dog peeps
from underneath his blanket.
Nothing penetrates his silent dream,

as I in limbo
drift.

Monday 16th
He's still in bed today,
morning almost spent,
beneath his sheets
he's unaware,
no cares intrude his sleep.
Rain outside is unimportant
in his shrunken world,
no worry for hay days,
or bailer-waiting,
no searching clouds,
no rushing to be done,
those days are gone.

Monday 30th
How do I carry on
with such a weight of mental pain?
Knowing he will never
journey home again.
He will never stride
his well-worn paths,
or laugh and chat with passing folk.
He will never tend his fallen walls,
his tools lie idle now,
no cow rests in the byre.
His fire is all burnt out.

Towards the end of July, Pauline encouraged me to see the doctor. I was only sleeping fitfully and there were the continual tears. He was really kind and understanding and we had a long chat. Was I depressed or sad? He said he felt I needed a course of antidepressants and sent me off with sympathy, pills and a form to complete.

As I clutched my pills, I felt a fraud; anyone would feel miserable in a situation like this. I could expect to feel sad, but clinically depressed?

At home I filled in the form, it was a range of questions.

1. Are you feeling down and weepy? Yes
2. Do you have a lack of ability to concentrate? Yes
3. Are you having difficulty in enjoying the things you normally do? Well, I feel guilty if I start to enjoy myself, so I guess that's a Yes.
4. Are you feeling tired for no reason? Yes
5. Are you comfort eating? Sadly another Yes
6. Are you feeling uncomfortable with people? Apart from close friends, that's a Yes
7. Are you finding it difficult to settle to do anything? I keep busy, but sometimes I can't remember what I've been busy with. I go on automatic, so I suppose that's a Yes
8. Are you feeling restless and at times doing too much? Chalk up another Yes
I decided that was quite a list. Perhaps I did need the pills.

One day Pauline and I went clothes shopping in Carlisle. I'd decided I needed a new wardrobe. It sounds extravagant but there was logic behind it. All my existing clothes held memories; I'd bought many of them when Eddie and I were going on holiday. We'd go shopping together, me laughing and saying, 'I can wear this on the ship,' or 'This will come in grand for the coach.' In typical man-fashion, Eddie would have been content with a change of socks and shirt but I did get him educated into holiday outfits. I had accumulated many knock-about, relax-in, happy-holiday clothes, but these clothes were now worn on my almost-daily visits to Eddie. Because of this, I felt they'd changed from happy to sad garments.

Once home, I set about dividing clothes. All the new garments – blouses, trousers and skirts – went into the empty wardrobe where Eddie's shirts and suits used to hang. My other clothes remained in my main wardrobe, isolated from the new ones. These were my survival clothes, segregated in their Silverdown box. Was I becoming paranoid?

My new clothes held no taint of Silverdown; they were to be worn for days out, evening meetings, church, in fact anything unconnected with my silent sad vigils or meaningless conversations. These clothes would not conjure memories of my beloved husband hiding under a blanket.

To emphasise the importance of this division of apparel, on my next visit to Eddie, a number of the residents were playing up. Eddie was obsessed that day about football; he was sorting out his team to play against America. While he pondered on who he would choose, Vic, who was sitting next to him, was finishing his lunch. Maisie walked over in an especially bad mood and decided to take Vic's pudding and custard. He swore and made a grab for the plate. She promptly emptied the lot over him, Eddie and I receiving a splash in the ensuing mayhem. Eddie, unaware of anything untoward, said, 'I want both of them on the team.'

That evening I went to a WI event and got into conversation with a lady I knew slightly. Her husband had died some years before of dementia. I suppose she was trying to be helpful as she described his final few months. He'd lived into the end stages and was bedridden, unable to speak or even swallow. I felt physically sick as I drove home; please God, spare Eddie from that! I didn't sleep much that night.

The glorious 12th was the Silverdown Fete. Many of the staff and relatives had been making craft items for the stall. I'd baked a cake and helped serve on the well-laden stall. It was a beautiful day and the enclosed garden had been laid out with tables, chairs and a few stalls. The money raised was used for special treats for the patients and was also put towards Christmas. Quite a few of the ambulant patients pottered around. Sadly Eddie took no part but slept in his chair throughout the afternoon.

By Monday 20th, the antidepressants were starting to have some affect. I was sleeping a little better and, to a certain extent, the tears had dried up. Eddie was very alert when I arrived. He'd been washing a cow, then we had to attend his auntie's funeral. 'She was really kind to me,' he said sadly, as we stood at the graveside. 'And she was no age.'

Some relatives arrived to see Sam; to Eddie, they were farming friends that we knew. 'How you doing?' Eddie shouted. 'Calf prices were good today. I topped the market.'

He noticed one of the carers nearby. 'She's come into money,' Eddie confided. 'Poor lass, she didn't used to have much but now she's flush. I hope she looks after it.' Changing track, he took my hand. 'Everything costs so much. Are you managing?'

I assured him I was.

He looked across to where Jessie was sitting, a toy dog under her chair. 'That dog's dead,' he said, patting Misty who lay on his knee. 'We'll have to bury it in the garden.'

Jessie got up, shoulder bag clutched protectively to her side as usual. 'What does she carry around?' Eddie asked.

'It's her money.'

'It's a good job she's looking after it. There's thieves

everywhere, you can't leave anything lying around.' Suddenly he lost interest, decided Misty was cold and needed wrapping up. Contented, as the dog was buried in a deep roll of blanket, he fell asleep.

CHAPTER 11

AUTUMN

Wednesday 3rd October was Eddie's eightieth birthday. I'd talked to the staff a week or so before, and it was agreed we'd hold a birthday party in one of the side sitting rooms. I'd sent out fifteen invitations. I'd mainly chosen family and friends that he'd known for many years. I decided that fifteen was about the limit, as I didn't want him over faced. I'd been into town and bought him a pink shirt and a navy jumper. On the Tuesday I'd put his birthday outfit on a hanger and the staff knew to dress him in them the next morning.

The day dawned and I was there for 1pm. His guests were due an hour later. The evening before I'd been worried that he would be having one of his many sleepy days and that the party would flow by without him noticing or taking part. When I arrived, it seemed as if my worries were justified as Eddie was under his blanket, sound asleep. When I tried to wake him he was grumpy. The staff said he'd slept all morning.

Around 1.25, I managed to stir him and he pulled the blanket down. 'Hello,' I said. 'Happy birthday.'

To my surprise his face lit up. 'October 3rd,' he declared.

He'd already received a number of cards, including mine and one from the staff. He leafed through them, smiling and enjoying the pictures, especially ones of horses. Then he needed the toilet and two of the carers supported him.

232

Afterwards they walked him through into the party room.

Silverdown had done us proud. The room was set out for his guests with birthday balloons; they'd also put on an amazing buffet at no extra cost. There were sandwiches, sausage rolls, cheese, biscuits and crisps, with three trifles, a Black Forest Gateau and even a birthday cake. I was overwhelmed by their kindness.

Shortly before two, Eddie's guests started to arrive: his sister Ruby and one of her sons, other relatives, friends and neighbours. All brought cards and went over and wished him a happy birthday. I was thrilled to see how alert he was, smiling and chatting, with a few tears.

I spoke to all the guests, asking them if they would take turns at sitting with Eddie so he had a chance to speak to them all. With so many familiar faces, it must have tweaked his memory as they joked and reminisced together. It was the best I'd seen him for months and Arty, who'd been coming most weeks, was happy and amazed to find him so bright.

Everyone helped themselves to the food and we lit the one candle on his cake. With a little help Eddie blew it out and everyone sang 'Happy Birthday'. There were party poppers, more cards, and lots of chat and laughter. Eddie said, 'It was the best birthday ever.'

Around four o'clock, his guests started to slip away. Eddie tried to struggle to his feet to see them off. We persuaded him to stay in his chair and he received lots of hugs, handshakes and kisses as they left. It was a lovely, joyful day, a day I will always treasure.

I was relieved that everything had gone so well. But there were a few guests there who had only seen him once or twice since he'd been admitted and I couldn't help wondering what they thought of me. To them, Eddie must have appeared older, frailer but otherwise little changed. Some must have gone away mystified as to why he was in the home, unable to understand why I hadn't been able to cope. This is the problem for anyone who finds themselves in a similar situation: the cartload of guilt is always lurking in the shadows.

When I visited the next day, Eddie was still quite bright and we looked through his cards again. The birthday balloon had been moved into his bedroom and the remains of the birthday cake were handed round at teatime.

'It was a lovely day yesterday. Did you enjoy seeing all your old friends?' I asked, as we sipped tea.

Eddie was pushing cake into his mouth, savouring the taste. 'Are they here?' he asked, looking round the day room, assessing the other patients.

'It was nice to see Ruby, and the others all here to celebrate your birthday,' I prompted. 'And the food was great.'

He looked at me, suddenly upset. 'Have I forgotten your birthday?'

'No, love, it was your birthday yesterday and you had that smashing party.'

He shook his head, brushing away the tears. 'Don't be daft. My birthday's not at Christmas,' he indicated the pile of cards. 'But we must go somewhere nice for your birthday.'

'That's a great idea.' We spent the remainder of teatime deciding where he'd like to take me and settled on Australia, so he could see their Ruby.

It was the annual harvest supper for the church in the market hall on Monday 8th. I went along to help and took a pudding I'd made. Everyone was very chatty and I had a good evening, but I couldn't help remembering that the previous year it had fallen on Eddie's birthday and they had all sung for him. It was so sad, the difference a year could bring.

The month drifted away with little change, as so many

months had. I continued to visit most days, always feeling at fault if a day passed and I didn't go. Sometimes I resolved to stay at home or go shopping, only to find myself off to Silverdown like a homing pigeon. When I was there I often sat in silence, fighting the distress which lay permanently beneath the surface; when I wasn't there, I yearned to see him. At times it was like a physical ache.

One day, when I was sitting by my sleeping husband, his hand resting limply in mine, I could hear one of the female patients calling from the television room. This was a pleasant room overlooking the garden and Eddie and I often sat there. It could seat around ten and there was a large television in one corner which was usually kept on, the sound turned low. Some of the patients liked to watch the changing pictures. This was the second television they'd had to replace since I'd been coming; one had been dragged off the wall by a resident and the other had received the unwanted attention of a jug of water.

'Alfred Parkinson! Are you there, Alfred Parkinson?' the voice demanded. She was seated just inside the doorway, directly in my line of vision, a well-wrinkled lady of around eighty, shrunken and tiny against the armchair. Her grey hair was still quite thick and curly; she must have had glorious locks in her youth.

A claw-like hand grasped at the air as she called again and again: 'Are you there, Alfred Parkinson?' But he never came, only a carer to bring her a drink and tuck a woolly blanket over her knees.

***

How I wish that Alfred Parkinson would come,
she calls for him all day,

but he stays away,
most likely dead,
he only lives within her head.
Eddie sleeps a lot these days,
I drift inside some waking daze
where nothing's real.
Maisie staggers by, her agonised expression
deep into her worried face,
she knows not place, or self or past,
I wonder how long she'll last?
Ivy shows off her yellow blouse,
and Elsie cries as Charlie comes to visit –
'Please take me home!'
Jessie moans as usual,
Eddie twitches in his sleep,
'Are you there, Alfred Parkinson?'

The 5th of November was the planned review of Eddie's condition to decide if he would still qualify for Continuing National Health Funding. I was on pins as I sat with him. Should the decision go against us, we'd be back to self-funding until Eddie's share of our savings was reduced. Then, unless I could somehow come up with the money, I would have to put our farm land on the market. I've said before how much this hurt. I'm sure some people reading this will say it's only right to have to sell an asset to pay for your care, and perhaps they're right – but the land rent was my main source of income for the future and to me it was a part of Eddie. A farm is part of the farmer, and the farmer is at one with his land.

I was called into the upper office. The same social worker was present with one of the nurses from the home but a different NHS nurse. She was kind but dispassionate, merely doing her job, laying out the case at it stood, being guided by the rules.

Eddie's file was open on the table and the various points were ticked off.

'No, he's not blacking out any more, that's down from severe to low, and he's eating better and has gained some weight.' I wanted to point out this was only because of the constant encouragement of the staff and myself. 'He's stopped having hallucinations, he just gets upset and worried occasionally. He's very placid most of the time.'

I wanted to shout, 'But he sleeps more and more,' but it didn't matter: that point went down from severe to low. I sat there in gathering panic and honestly wondered if I was going to vomit or faint. I felt at that moment as if I'd had a win on the lottery only to discover it was a mistake, or I'd lost the ticket. I'd been convinced, as Eddie gradually failed, that once the funding was granted it could not be withdrawn.

'He's fallen twelve times since June,' said the nurse from the home.

Yes, that was true; I'd had a lot of phone calls. He could still manage to struggle to his feet then he was down before a carer could reach him. It seemed a worrying number of falls but most were more slump than fall; thankfully the worst injuries he'd suffered were two minor cuts and a few bruises. They mainly happened in the day room, which had a special soft, cushioned floor. I'd been alarmed at times but understood it was impossible for a carer to sit with him constantly. I also realised that if Eddie had still been at home I'd have faced the same problem, with the added complication of how to pick him up.

I was asked to leave while they discussed his case file. I went back downstairs; I must have looked shocked, as one of the carers brought me a cup of tea. 'Try not to worry,' she consoled. 'I'm sure he'll still qualify. I mean, look at him.'

I did as I sipped the hot tea, the tears threatening. I knew he'd gained a little weight but he had become a frail old man; the strong, agile farmer of just a couple of years before was gone forever. He might not be having hallucinations any more but his mind was a jumbled mess, his life memories thrown in the air and scattered like autumn leaves. He couldn't dress, wash, shave, shower or take his own medication, and he could only scramble along supported by two carers. He was doubly incontinent, could no longer write or read, and didn't know where he was or who I was most of the time. My thoughts were interrupted as I was called back to the office.

I tried to read their faces as I entered, feeling like a criminal at the bar, waiting for the jury to pronounce guilt or innocence. It was the NHS nurse who spoke. 'This time your husband still qualifies and his funding will be guaranteed for a year.' I think I let out the breath I'd been holding. 'But I have to warn you, he's borderline and is only eligible because of his high risk of falling,' she informed me. 'Should he go off his legs totally and be unable to stand, his fall risk would then be reduced from severe to low. If that occurs by next November, he will not have enough severe or high points to qualify and the funding will be withdrawn.'

My legs felt like rubber as I returned to sit with Eddie. We'd had a stay of execution but the threat had only been postponed. The illogical framework of the funding criteria made me feel bemused. If Eddie's condition had worsened by next year and he'd become bed- or chair-bound, he wouldn't be eligible for the funding.

I sat in a daze as he chatted, telling me he'd been busy making a gate for the top field. 'I had to pack in because it started raining but I must get it finished tomorrow. The cows are getting out into the lane. Are you ready to bottle?'

he asked, trying to get up.

I steadied him and he sank back into the chair, swaying against his cushions. I had to get away; the ordeal had been too much and my mind could stand no more for the time being.

'I've a few jobs to do around the house first,' I said, getting up. 'You finish your cake and have your chocolate.' I tore the wrapper off the milk chocolate bar and handed it to him. He took it, snapping off a large chunk and pushing it into his mouth with delight. I bent down, kissed his head and left, knowing that in a few minutes he would have forgotten I was ever there, forgotten about the gate and the cows and the bottling. He'd be away in his own illogical world where I could not go, and soon he would be asleep.

Not for the first or the last time, I didn't remember the drive home. God, I hate November! Eddie was diagnosed with vascular dementia in November 2010, he was admitted to Silverdown the following November. Next November was a year away, but the time would pass and it was there waiting, lurking in the cupboard of tomorrow.

I went to bed late, hoping I'd be so exhausted I might get some sleep. I did but I was awake by 5am. Further sleep was impossible and I was up by 6.30, wandering aimlessly around the house with a 'worry' headache.

I went to see Pauline later and told her all my troubles. Like me, she was astounded that Eddie might have his funding withdrawn if he grew worse. I visited him in the afternoon and talked to my neighbour Charlie in the evening. 'Don't worry,' he said. 'You're okay for a year. A lot can happen by next November.' That elephant was bumping around in the room again.

I'd received a letter a few weeks earlier inviting me to attend a focus group for research into the effects caring has on carers, with the object of implementing improvements. It had been commissioned by Cumbria County Council and was being held at the local hospital. I had pointed out that I was no longer a carer but, since I'd had recent experience, it appeared they still wanted my input.

There were around fourteen people present, mainly women in their sixties and seventies, and a couple of elderly men. I think this meeting must have been specially aimed at older carers, as I knew many young and middle-aged people were also devoting their lives to a family member. The meeting was chaired by a social worker who welcomed us all. Tea and biscuits were given out then we were each asked our experience of caring. When it was my turn, I said that I'd cared for my husband with vascular dementia at home for over a year but that he was now in a care home.

We were there for two hours, everyone highlighting the various problems they had encountered. The main difficulties seemed to revolve around the lack of home support and the isolation. Many said they couldn't have managed without regular help from family and friends and explained how tired they became.

As I listened, I recognised so many similar problems and challenges. I felt humbled by some of those present who were giving their final years, wearing themselves out looking after an ill relative. Not all were struggling to look after someone with dementia, many of their relatives had become incapacitated by strokes, Parkinson's Disease or other debilitating conditions. All of them had handed over their lives out of love or duty. One elderly lady especially left me with a feeling of intense failure and shame. She had been caring for her husband, who was suffering from Parkinson's and dementia, for twelve years. I asked how she carried on. 'It's a privilege,' she replied.

I felt bad as I left and headed to see Eddie. He was sleepy when I arrived but shortly afterwards had one of his strange 'turns'. He started to vomit then went ghostly white before becoming floppy and unconscious. The nurse and carers rushed to him as he slowly revived; the doctor was called and Eddie was put to bed.

I was sitting at his bedside when the doctor arrived. He decided Eddie's blood pressure had plunged and prescribed sleep and observation. I couldn't help thinking that this was now one of the areas where he'd been marked down as low. I wondered if this was the beginning of another cycle of blackouts.

I sat for two hours in the quiet room as the rain dashed against the window. Eddie's room overlooked the pathway leading to the main entrance and I watched staff scurrying back and forth and relatives coming and going. The only sounds were Eddie's heavy breathing and water hitting the glass, producing raindrops that ran down the window, blurring the view. One of the staff brought me a tray of tea with a piece of cake; they assured me they'd give Eddie something when he woke.

Who could have foretold?
Who could have supposed
In the darkest dreams,
In the darkest night?
That it would ever have come to this.
From the blond-haired boy at the village school,
Sunday prayer and pony rides.
To a man full grown,
And the farmer's life,
Loving parents then a wife,
Days of work in the cold and rain,

Tramping up the fields
Then back again,
The milking shed on a struggling dawn,
Problems calving, muck to spread,
Hay and silage, walls to mend.
Flowing years, then the farming ends.
A brief retirement, and wings to spread,
But new horizons and dreams have fled.
Forced to leave his home and land,
Now time drifts on as falling sand.
One consolation, he feels no pain,
Knows not he will never go home again.
Who could have imagined?
Who could have foretold?
The hand life dealt him,
When he grew old.

On the 10th November it was a year since Eddie had arrived at Silverdown. I don't suppose anyone but me remembered – who had any reason to? The year seemed to have been interminable and I'd drifted through it in a sort of limbo. At times I'd felt as if I were climbing a cliff, clinging on with my fingernails, about to fall at any second. The antidepressants had helped but I was only on a low dose and didn't want to become dependent on pills; they were a crutch, nothing more.

My state of mind was not improved by a second-hand conversation that was relayed to me by a friend. She'd been talking to someone and I'd come up in the conversation. The lady had laughed and said, 'Jackie's having a ball now Eddie's in a care home.'

There was no reply to this, no answer; if that was what she believed, all I could think was that I hoped she never had to deal with a similar situation.

It was the middle of November and the weather was atrocious, mainly heavy rain, but I had my winter tyres ready for the snow and ice when it came. Eddie had been in the same room since his arrival and I'd become used to it over the year; of course, Eddie was unaware of what it was like. He'd been an urgent admission and the room he was allocated had yet to be improved. I liked it in spite of its lack of modernity because it was spacious. It was clean, though obviously in need of some bright re-decoration. The furniture was of the older, heavy-wood variety, which could make the room appear dark even though the window was wide. I'd had plenty of wardrobe and drawer space to put all his clothes, and his small en suite contained a sizeable white wash-stand and toilet.

'Would you like Eddie moved into one of the upgraded rooms?' one of the male carers asked me one day. We went along to the opposite end of the downstairs floor, to a room which overlooked the enclosed garden. It was in the process of being decorated, with a colourful flowery wallpaper. The woodwork was newly painted and, even though the room was smaller, it had a large window and felt full of light, radiating a cheerful atmosphere.

'Next door was finished a few months ago. This room will look the same when it's completed.' We headed into the other room, which was the same size. Bright new curtains danced at the windows and the matching furniture was pale pine, adding to the light, airy feel. I loved it. We agreed that Eddie would be transferred as soon as the room was ready.

Little changed over the remainder of November apart from the weather growing worse. Eddie settled into his new surroundings with no trouble and, as I expected, he didn't notice. In his mind he wasn't there anyway; he was still at

The Mill, going about his daily farming work as normal.

We had some weird and wonderful chats on the days he was awake, one minute discussing the price of pigs and hoping that the newly farrowed sow didn't squash her young, the next deciding which chocolate bar he preferred. Then we'd be off to see Bobby and we'd talk about how well he was looking. We hoped we'd soon get to see Ruby in Australia. Eddie's mum came to visit and brought him a cake; he said how good it was to see her, especially as she was so busy on the farm and with her war work. We'd break off in the middle of this conversation because a load of straw had arrived and, as Eddie staggered to his feet with two carers supporting him, he'd struggle along the corridor to talk to the wagon driver. Back in his chair, he was freshly back from the auction market, satisfied that his bull calf had sold well.

Over the year, the other patients and their relatives had become a part of our journey. Once inside the doors of Silverdown, the real world closed behind me and I entered into the land of 'the care-home family'. Because of this, I noticed their deterioration; each patient, like Eddie, was declining, some faster than others. I ached for their relatives as a once-agitated but ambulant patient would be reduced to being chair-bound, unable to speak and in need of feeding; another would vanish upstairs where the bedridden patients were gently cared for as their lives ebbed away.

December arrived: could I really think of Christmas? This would be the third since Eddie was diagnosed. We'd bumbled through the first, he'd passed out during the second, and I had no idea what the third would bring.

I'd made the effort to buy my Christmas cards, compile a list and write them when I had the chance. As before, the staff made a special effort to dress the home in seasonal decorations and a large tree graced the main sitting room.

There were sing-songs, carols, various entertainers and as happy an atmosphere as was possible. Silverdown held their annual Christmas fete, and it was arranged that I would be there for Christmas dinner.

The staff were enthusiastic about the future; some had visited other homes and been on courses. They were bubbling with ideas of how to make additions to the home, to enhance the patients' experience and help stir memories. Each room was gradually being equipped with a 'memory box' on the wall outside. Relatives had been asked to bring photographs and items that held special life memories to put into these boxes. I was planning Eddie's box – pictures of his childhood, a toy cow, miniature tractor and perhaps a tiny motorbike to remind him of when he used to go to the Isle of Man TT races.

Other ideas in the pipeline were for imitation shop windows to be attached to some of the corridor walls. They were getting a joiner, husband to one of the staff, to do the woodwork. Relatives and staff were hunting out old items which could be displayed. 'We're going to have a vintage grocer's with tinned stuff and adverts from the past. Perhaps a sweet shop and general store,' I'd been told. 'Plus we're putting up a bus stop somewhere in the sitting room. Some of the patients are always on about catching the bus.' It all sounded positive, and I looked forward to seeing it all up and running. They already played gentle 1940s' and 50s' background music. The residents could regularly be seen humming and foot-taping, some joining in the words.

On Sunday 9th December, Eddie was asleep in his chair in the main day room. The nurse came over as I arrived and said he seemed to have developed a cold and was a bit chesty. I listened to his breathing as I sat beside him, picking up a low rattle with each breath. She said he'd had no breakfast and wouldn't take any fluids, but they would keep trying. They put him back to bed mid-afternoon and I stayed with him until five; he never woke but his chest seemed quieter. I decided to slip home for a few hours and come back later.

I phoned at 7pm. They had sent for Q Doc (the out-of-hours emergency doctor). The nurse thought Eddie should be seen and given antibiotics and any other treatment required. 'Don't worry,' she said. 'It's mainly a precaution in case he suddenly becomes worse during the night.'

I decided to head back there then I'd know what the doctor had said. I'd most likely stay the night if needed. I was just getting ready to set off when the phone rang. It was the nurse; the doctor had come, given Eddie no treatment but was insisting he be sent to hospital. The ambulance had been booked.

In rising panic, I jumped in the car; the journey usually took me about twenty minutes but I did it in fifteen and hurried to Eddie's room on arrival. He was conscious but a little sleepy. His breathing was little changed from earlier but he was sweaty, possibly due to a raised temperature. 'I really don't want him to go to hospital but to be treated here,' I said. 'It was supposed to be put in his GP notes.'

'We have it recorded as well,' the nurse assured me, 'but the doctor wouldn't listen.'

'Is he still here?' I asked.

'You might catch him, he just went out to his car.' It was a bitter night as I dashed outside to see a thin, grey-haired man carrying a bag getting into the driver's seat. Since he was parked in the bay reserved for visiting health professionals, I assumed he was the doctor. I hurried to the car and tapped on the window. I'd never met him before.

I was greeted by a cold frown. Reluctantly he lowered the window.

'I'm Mrs Huck, you've just seen my husband. In view of his dementia, I don't want him to go to hospital.' I was about to explain what had been agreed with the casualty consultant and the home when he cut me off.

'I've referred him to hospital, that's the end of it!' The window was shut and, without another word or backward glance, he drove off.

The first flakes of thin wispy snow illuminated by the outside light drifted down, their wet touch brushing my cheek. For a few seconds I stood on the path, stunned into immobility. All the worry of Eddie's previous trip to Carlisle came rushing back, especially his inability to understand where he was or what was going on. Was I wrong to demand he stay at Silverdown? Should I be thankful that the doctor had decided his condition warranted specialist care? I was in turmoil as I headed back inside to await the ambulance.

The staff had packed him an overnight bag, hoping it wouldn't be needed. They said that possibly, after an assessment, treatment and one-night stay, he would be returned. It was 10.15 when the ambulance arrived; they came in with a trolley and prepared him for the drive. I chatted to the ambulance men, explaining my reasons for him staying at Silverdown.

'Do you want to speak to our controller? they asked.

I was put through and once more explained that my husband was in the advanced stages of dementia, was very confused, in danger of falling if not watched constantly, and that any necessary treatment he needed should have and could have been given at the home. The controller was very kind and understanding but stressed that since the doctor had ordered his transfer to hospital, they had to carry out his instructions.

Eddie was by now was fairly alert. 'Are we going to see

our Bobby?' he asked the ambulance men as they prepared him for the journey. 'It's a while since I was at Melton. He's been living in Australia but he's home now.'

So off we went through the dark, wintery night to Carlisle. I set off first, knowing they would get there faster than me. I ran through a range of emotions as I drove: angry, then desperate, worried sick, afraid and helpless.

What if they wanted to admit Eddie? Would the staff grasp the additional care he needed? I knew he would be looked after by trained staff but would they have the time to give him the individual attention he needed? He couldn't explain what he wanted or how he felt; he was doubly incontinent, almost off his legs and totally unable to comprehend what was said or where he was.

I beat the ambulance by five minutes and met them pushing Eddie on the trolley through the main door. I was surprised he was not going to A&E but was being sent directly to the general admissions ward. I followed, carrying his bag, my footsteps echoing over the floor of the silent corridor. The usual ceaseless bustle of the hospital by day was replaced by a sterile silence.

We arrived at the ward where the ambulance men were directed to a bed that had been made up. Two members of staff came in while I was asked to wait outside. Ten minutes later, I was allowed to re-join them. They'd done various readings and one was busy filling in a chart. Eddie was sleepy again but had taken no hurt on the unexpected drive to Carlisle.

The registrar came to see him half an hour later. This time I was allowed to stay as he was examined. The doctor listened to his chest before turning to me.

'He's got a chest infection which, if untreated, could rapidly become broncho-pneumonia.' He re-read the letter which had been sent with Eddie before looking up. 'As you're aware, he's in an advanced stage of dementia with all the associated problems. We could give him oxygen if needed, make him comfortable and let nature take its course, or I could put up a drip and give him intravenous antibiotics. What do you want me to do?'

CHAPTER 12

WINTER

LASTING LOVE

I loved you first in spring,
I met your smile
While unaware that
You were there,
Another glance, we danced,
Your work-cracked palm in mine,
And so it all began
I'd found my man.

My love grew deeper in the summer heat,
In harmony as one
We coasted on, complete.
A million memories shared
You cared so much for me,
Love filled my soul,
And made me whole.

We shared the autumn
Of comfortable content
God sent,
Easy words and knowing,
Showing love in lots of little ways
Our ship sailed onwards
Through the tranquil days -

And when the winter comes
As come it must,
My trust in you will never wane,
Together or alone
You'll always be my own,
Our pilot-light shines bright,
From spring to winter,
From dawn, down to
The endless night.

The seconds ticked away as I held Eddie's hand. The words of the lady whose husband had died after suffering the final stages of dementia rang in my mind. 'At the end, he was completely helpless. He didn't know anyone, couldn't speak, he couldn't even swallow.' If Eddie lived, was that what was waiting for him in the next weeks or months? Christmas was coming; surely he couldn't die before Christmas?

I remembered Charlie's words: 'It's a long time before next November.' I seemed to spin in uncertainty. The registrar waited; it felt like time itself waited.

But I knew I couldn't let him go. I wasn't ready: would I ever be ready?

'Put up the drip,' I said.

I stayed until the early hours of the morning. By then Eddie was in a deep sleep, the drip established in his arm and his breathing coming with less difficulty.

'Why don't you go home and get some sleep?' one of the nurses urged. 'Now he's asleep, he most likely won't wake until morning. Try not to worry, we'll take care of him.'

For now, my anxiety and uncertainty regarding his care allayed, I decided to trust them. They had been thorough since his admission and had been coming to his bedside regularly. I was exhausted – and who knew what the day would bring? So I kissed him and left, driving past the new snow on my return home.

Monday 10th December: a day of desperation and unease. I phoned the ward at 8am; they had no information and didn't appear to know who I was enquiring about. After pressing them, I was informed he was okay. 'Phone back after 11am,' I was told.

I phoned Pauline and we agreed to go to the hospital and get some answers; she would pick me up at noon. I rang the ward as arranged at 11am; they were keeping him in to administer the antibiotics, but he was very confused! Good grief, of course he was confused – he was suffering from advanced dementia!

Pauline picked me up and we dropped in at Silverdown to see what they felt about the situation. The nurse in charge said they were happy to have him back as soon as possible, and would give him whatever treatment was prescribed, so we drove on to Carlisle.

I try not to criticise the NHS. Where would we be without it? I know it's not perfect – what organisation is? – but it's a lifeline in time of need. It is mainly staffed by hardworking, dedicated professionals who do their best, often in difficult circumstances. I know, I've been there. When it works well it is a godsend, but at times it leaves room for improvement.

When we arrived on the ward, which was the main admission catchpoint for the hospital, it resembled a railway station at rush hour. Everyone seemed to be on the move, nurses of all designations flowed backwards and forwards. Not being accustomed to the uniforms, all the different ranks looked the same to me, unlike when I worked in hospital where no one could fail to pick out the sister or charge nurse. Added to the nurses was a variety of other staff who could have been anything from porters to cleaners. Of one thing I was sure: there couldn't possibly be a shortage of staff on this ward. Half the hospital appeared to be here.

We asked about Eddie after not finding him in the bed he'd been allocated on admission. The nurse I asked, who was mid-stride, looked bemused, eventually pointing out a six-bedded bay halfway down the ward. 'You won't be able to go in,' she said, 'there's an infection in there and it's cordoned off.'

Pauline and I looked at each other, appalled, but the nurse had gone before we could ask any further questions.

The open end of the bay was roped off with a red 'NO ADMISSION' sign pinned on it. We looked in; Eddie was in the first bed on the right, obviously either semi-conscious or asleep. He was curled under a single sheet in the foetal position, lying on his side, hardly the best position for someone with a chest infection. I presumed his arm, which was hidden under the sheet, was attached to the drip that was at his bedside and nearly empty. His mouth was open as he strained for breath, a dry crust forming on his lips. He hadn't been shaved and his hair hung damp across his brow. He looked terrible.

Pauline put a comforting arm around me as I struggled for control. I knew I didn't want Eddie to die here; if he had to die, I wanted him back in his bright, peaceful room at Silverdown. I wanted him surrounded by the love, care and kindness he had received since his admission. I wanted him to die with dignity, even if he knew nothing about it.

Another nurse was hurrying past. 'Would it be possible to speak to the sister?' I asked.

'She's busy at the moment with the consultant's ward round.'

'Could I speak to the consultant?'

'You'll have to ask Sister,' and she was gone.

We stood outside the bay where Eddie was, watching the slow progress of the consultant and his posse of junior doctors. He was working his way gradually up the left-hand bays, which meant that he wouldn't reach the bay where Eddie was for some considerable time.

I've worked with doctors of all ranks and in the past was used to dealing with both medical specialists and high-brow surgeons. As the group drew parallel I decided to seize the moment. 'Excuse me,' I said politely. 'Could I have a few words with you about my husband, Edwin Huck?'

He spun round, giving me a look reserved for something disgusting he'd picked up on his shoe. He was a small, middle-aged man, most likely overloaded with work, extremely busy and possibly just downright bad mannered. 'If you want to speak to me,' he snapped, 'you'll have to make an appointment!' I was upset enough to explode, but I knew I would have dissolved into tears, so I gave him what I hoped was a withering look.

'Well, thank you for all your help,' I said, as I turned away back to Pauline.

We were determined not to leave the outside of Eddie's bay until something had been resolved. I suppose there was a relatives' room, though no one had told us where it was, and I didn't want us to be sitting in there and miss the chance of speaking to someone about Eddie. No one offered us chairs or tea; no one enquired why we were standing there; we might have been invisible.

For the next hour and a half we were ignored by the milling herd of passing staff. During my years of nursing, I hope I never unwittingly treated relatives in this manner. I know we can all be overwhelmed with work but I'm certain that in a similar situation in the past either the sister or one of the nurses would have asked if they could help. During our wait no one went into Eddie's bay to check on him, offer him fluids, attend to his drip (which was now empty) or clean his mouth.

Finally a junior doctor and the sister came to speak to us. I explained about wanting him to be returned to Silverdown, where his treatment could continue; in view of his dementia this was the best place for him. They seemed rather restrained; the sister a shadow of the strong, dominant matriarchs of the past. They would pass my words onto the consultant. Like rabbits they scuttered away.

Finally the consultant reached Eddie's bay. Disregarding any attempt at quarantine, the rope having been removed, he and his retinue piled in. Still we waited as he worked his way through the patients. Eddie was the last one he saw and the curtains were drawn round as he was examined. At last they emerged, the consultant in the lead. After all this wait, there was no way he was going to get past me.

His tone was more conciliatory; possibly he was guilty at his hasty and rude dismissal of me, or perhaps he was worried I might complain. People do these days. Or it could have merely been that I'd misjudged him and he was overworked and tired, and he'd put me down as an interfering, over-anxious relative who just couldn't wait until he'd finished his rounds.

'Your husband is extremely ill,' he said. 'I think there is little chance of his recovery. We've really done all we can for him. The care home is prepared to have him back?'

'Yes, as soon as possible.'

'Well, we do need the bed. I'll arrange his discharge this evening.' And that was that; he had more on his mind than me and Eddie. We were dismissed as he carried on with the remainder of his round.

Even though the doctors had been allowed into the bay, visitors were still banned. Now I knew Eddie would soon be on his way back to Silverdown, my mind eased a little. Now my main worry was how ill he was; would he make it back to the home?

Pauline and I were discussing what to do next when two nurses entered Eddie's bay. Again the curtains were drawn; thankfully, when they were pulled back, his bed had been made, he'd been changed and his mouth cleaned and a fresh drip bottle instated. He still hadn't been sat up or shaved but it was a start, and he'd be back at Silverdown in a few hours.

It was late afternoon by now and I expected that arrangements must be in hand for his transfer. 'Let's go back to Silverdown and wait for him,' I said to Pauline; she agreed and we headed out.

I'll never know what happened that night. I set off optimistic but, when we reached Silverdown, my hopes were dashed. I was told they'd had a phone call from the hospital: Eddie would be staying the night as they wanted to continue the intravenous antibiotics.

Why couldn't these be administered by the trained nursing staff at the home? No one knew the answer. Why had the consultant gone back on what he'd told me? What should I do – dash back to Carlisle? Not for the first time in this journey, I was left upset and uncertain. If I did go back to the ward, I couldn't sit with him. Surely if he took a turn for the worse they would phone me; they had both my home and mobile number. Eventually Pauline persuaded me to go back to hers, she'd make a meal.

I phoned at eight and ten but there was no change. I passed an uneasy night, sleeping fitfully, waking to worry. I phoned again at 9am the next morning; at eleven I managed to speak to the nurse who was caring for him. He'd pulled out his intravenous cannula a few times but he was comfortable and sleeping.

I felt he was now simply being left to die and, if this was the case, I wanted that to happen at Silverdown. It was agreed that I could have an 'ethical' discussion with the doctor when I arrived at the hospital.

I drove to Pauline, had one of my many howls all over her, then we went to Carlisle. We spoke to a junior doctor shortly after we arrived. 'He's pulled the IV out a few times,' he said. 'Unless you're insistent it be reinstated, I think we should leave him in peace and let nature take its course.'

'Can he be transferred back to Silverdown?'

'Yes, if that's what you'd prefer.'

So at last it was sorted. I still couldn't go in to sit with Eddie. When I looked in, he was propped up in bed and had been shaved. He slept, oblivious to all my worry. I could almost hear him say with a laugh, 'Don't fuss yourself, lass. I'll be fine.'

It was 6pm when we arrived back at Silverdown. They were expecting him, but he hadn't yet arrived. Pauline took me home and I collapsed, exhausted, on the sofa. The home would phone as soon as Eddie turned up.

For the next few hours I drifted, feeling suspended in space. I rang Ruby to tell her what had happened and prepare her for the worst. Thoughts wouldn't come; I watched the television, but nothing registered. I might have slept, I don't know. I was too tired to light the Rayburn so managed with the electric fire, still feeling cold. The cats curled around me for comfort and I ran my fingers through their warm fur.

The ambulance brought Eddie back to Silverdown at 9pm. I spoke to the nurse in charge, asking her if I should come. 'He's deeply asleep, Jackie,' she said. 'His breathing is much better. The antibiotics must have done some good. If there's any change in the night I'll ring you. Try to get some sleep.'

I phoned early; he'd had a peaceful night. After sorting the essentials, I drove to Silverdown and was soon seated in his room. A weak winter sun shone from the garden, dancing on the bright curtains and wallpaper. Eddie was sitting up in bed washed, shaved, in his own pyjamas and, to my astonishment, the staff said they'd had him sat on the edge of the bed and he'd drunk two glasses of pineapple and orange, his favourite.

I stayed all day, glad to see his colour had improved and his breathing was easier. The nurse and other carers came in regularly to change him as needed and give him fluids. He was still very sleepy, but able to sip the liquid when it was offered.

At last my mind was at rest. He was back where his condition was understood, and he would receive the one-to-one care he required. He was no longer in an impersonal, infected hospital ward, but in his own room surrounded by his own things.

I was still convinced that the treatment he'd received in hospital could have been administered at Silverdown, without all the turmoil of a hospital admission. Was he going to die? I didn't know. At the moment his condition had improved but this could be temporary; whatever happened I could be at his side.

The GP (a different one from the Q Doc) came to see him and was happy with the improvement. We had a talk and it was agreed that Eddie was not to go back to Carlisle and, if he collapsed, not to be resuscitated. Does that sound cruel, unfeeling, uncaring? Or kind and practical? It's a terrible place to find yourself in alone with no one to share the decision. If we'd had children, they would have been there to agree or protest but there was just me. I hoped everyone would understand I was doing this for Eddie out of love. There was no hope for the future, no chance of mental or physical improvement. It was a downhill descent, with no stopping.

Our local vicar came to see us in the afternoon. She was genuine and considerate. She prayed for us while Eddie slept. I stayed until early evening. There had been little change but I would be informed at once if I was needed.

Another night, another day. My mind was in a strange place: I'd prepared myself for Eddie to die but now there was a chance he would live. We'd see Christmas, welcome 2013 in together – who knows, we might see spring and beyond. I started to grasp at hope for more time together and went back to preparing his 'memory box'. I gave Christmas preparations another thought, wondering what I could buy Eddie. A new CD for him to listen to? Perhaps I could find another horse picture book?

He was dressed and sitting out of bed the next morning and more alert. He'd had some porridge and taken tea and a soft drink. Again I stayed all day; this time when he woke he knew I was there and stroked my hand until he fell asleep. Ruby and one of her sons came to see him. I was so glad, though I know it upset them. If Eddie should die, I wouldn't have wanted it to happen without them seeing each other one final time.

Little changed over the next two days. I stayed with him each day. He slept a lot of the time. The staff got him up for a few hours but put him back to bed when he seemed tired. He ate a little and drank a good amount of fluids. He looked wizened and was extremely weak but he was alive, in no pain, warm and well-cared for.

To my great distress, on Monday 17th December I had

an early-morning call from Silverdown. Eddie's condition was unchanged but the home was once again locked down in quarantine because a few of the patients had contracted norovirus. I understood the problems of keeping infection at bay with a steady stream of visitors and staff, and did not underestimate the problems of cross-infection from the patients themselves, but to be separated from Eddie at a time when his life might be ebbing away was almost unbearable. If he deteriorated I would be able to go; otherwise, as with other visitors, I was barred. All I could do was wait, worry and phone at regular intervals.

It was Wednesday 19th. I rang early. No change; he'd had a good night and they were in the process of getting him up. They'd had no new cases and visiting should recommence in a day or two.

That morning I'd agreed to go to the village drop-in Christmas meeting. I'd been asked to read a few of my Christmas poems and there were going to be carols and mince pies. I sat and chatted to Pauline, other villagers and WI friends and, just for a short while, I relaxed and enjoyed the prospect of Christmas.

I was out a little over an hour but the phone was ringing as I walked through the door. It was Silverdown. 'Jackie, can you come at once? Eddie's taken a turn for the worse and we think you should be here.'

My hands started to shake. Was this it? Was this the end?

I popped back in the car to the drop-in; most people were still there. Pauline could see something had happened. 'They've sent for me, Eddie's worse,' I told her.

'Do you want me to come with you?' she asked.

No. In a strange way, I had to do this last lap alone. If this was the end of the journey, I wanted it to be just me and Eddie, the way we had begun. If he did die, I had no idea how I would feel and no amount of comfort from anyone was going to help.

'I'll let you know what happens,' I said as I left, seeing the news being passed around. Soon the whole village would know.

As soon as I saw Eddie, I knew he wouldn't be long. His breathing came in short rattling gasps and he was unconscious. I phoned Ruby and Pauline with an update. I also phoned another friend to ask her to feed the cats, and the WI secretary to explain I wouldn't be there that evening. It was the WI Christmas party, a highlight of our year, but this year it would have to go on without me.

The staff were thoughtful and kind, bringing me food and drink and coming back and forth to continue their loving care. I tried to read a book but mainly just sat beside his bed as his life slipped away.

As I watched and waited, memories and pictures floated in my mind. I thought back to our wedding day; how handsome he'd been in his hired dress suit. Our honeymoon in Wales, all the new places I'd been able to show Eddie; even when the tide had nearly taken the car, we'd laughed so much. All the years in between, the early holidays to Devon and the Norfolk Broads. Picnics, long happy walks, meandering and motoring on quiet lanes. Hay time and the fight to get the hay safely in the barn before the weather changed, and the frustration when the baler broke down. Fighting our way out on winter mornings to deliver the milk, Eddie saying, 'It should be a pound a pint on these days.' Getting stuck in the snow and having to ask a local farmer to pull us out, pushing and shovelling but, 'The milk must get through'.

There was one morning, as we were going under the motorway bridge, that we saw a life-size dinosaur travelling overhead. It must have been on a low-loader but it just looked as if it were flying over our heads. Another time, there had been the most tremendous storm and we sat in the house waiting to go out and heard the garage roof rattling away down the yard.

And always there were cows. Eddie walking the fields to bring the cows in for milking; Eddie in the milking shed moving from animal to animal, patting them in his own gentle way to encourage them to relax and 'let their milk down'. Cows calving, cows needing the vet, cows going to market. I'll always remember going into the cowshed on a winter's evening; the cows had been milked and were being bedded down in their stalls. The warmth glowed from them as they stood or knelt down with that regular contented sound of chewing cud.

The final memories were of our wonderful holidays after Eddie retired. I smiled as I pictured him lying round the pool on one of our Mediterranean cruises. There he would be as the sun beat down, resplendent in mole-skin trousers, shirt, tie and jumper. 'Aren't you hot?' I'd ask, as men with big bellies hanging over swimming trunks waddled past.

'I might just take off my tie,' he'd say. An hour later the jumper would follow, but nothing more. One day I remembered his pants riding up, leaving two white areas of flesh. Eddie had very fair skin and developed blisters on both legs just above his ankles. Over the next day they came up like miniature balloons. He was so proud of them and, amazingly, never complained they were sore.

On formal nights, how smart he'd looked in his dress suit with frilled shirt and bow tie. He always said on those occasions, 'I don't care what I eat, as long as it's not red and drippy!'

All those places we went, those amazing sights: Rome, Pisa, Paris, Amsterdam, Venice, Malta and so much more.

I remembered Gibraltar and the Barbary apes. Eddie was fascinated. We watched a real cheeky creature dash into the gift shop and return with a handful of chocolate bars. It leapt up high onto a wall and, as we watched, shared its stolen plunder round the family.

The day staff went off duty at 8.30. Before leaving, they came in, kissed Eddie goodbye and hugged me.

I saw Santa on my way today
He crossed the road and waved –
nice chap. I've saved my tears
for later.
You're breathing at a gallop in short bursts,
silence, then you start again.
I wander in my thoughts,
hear your voice,
feel your touch,
but you've already gone
just your heart beats on.
The road's seemed long yet short,
but as we near the end
I give my love and thanks
to you my sweetheart and my friend.
I'll carry you for always in my heart,
we'll never really part.

The night-staff continue their devoted care. At 11.30 they put a mattress on the carpet for me with pillow and sheets, install a lamp and switch off the main light. I lie there sleepless, listening, waiting, counting. Midnight: your breaths come at sixty, seventy a minute.

At 2.20 they alter, gradually becoming slower. I remove the mattress, pull up a chair and sit by your bedside, holding your damp hand. You know nothing; you die as you have lived, peacefully. The latest Misty lies near the foot of your bed but the staff have placed a small stuffed dog on your pillow to watch over you. Gradually, oh so gradually, your breathing slows. One of the nurses slips in, feels your pulse and presses a comforting hand on my shoulder, then leaves us alone.

Eddie died at 2.40am on 20th December 2012.

The train slowed to a stop
Leaving silence
So in peace
The journey ends.

Postscript

Silverdown Care Home closed just under a year after Eddie died. It was the only purpose-built home for dementia sufferers in the area. There are plans to turn it into houses.